Master in a Minute®

SUNFLOWERS

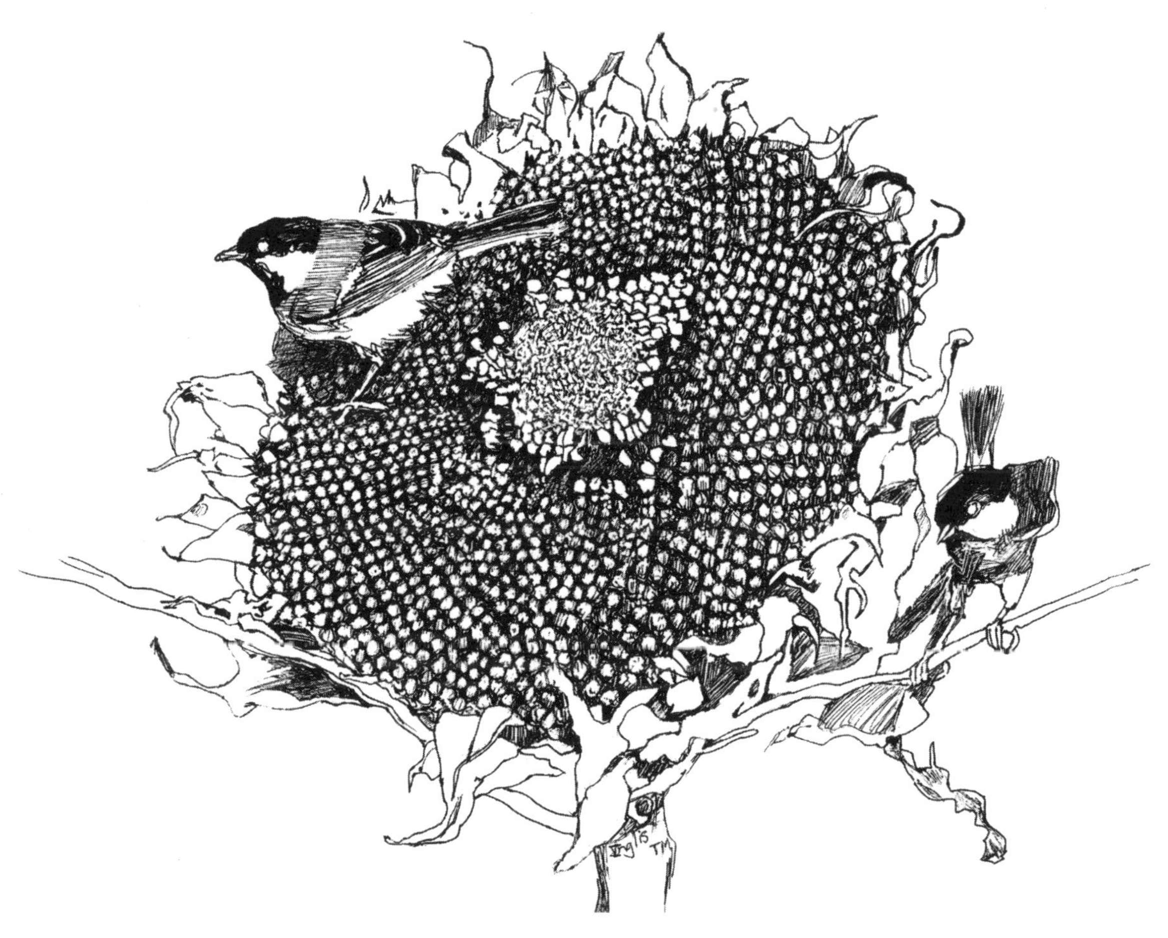

JENNET INGLIS ™

ISBN: 978-0-9884470-4-2

Dragon Hill Publishers LLC, Staunton, Virginia, USA
www.dragonhillpublishers.com

Cover and Interior Design by Mayapriya Long of Bookwrights
Editing by ParvatiM LLC

Dedication

This very minute, now, it's you.
Steady on. Find your magic.

A life may be far less than grand,
But may be transformed in a moment you see,
By The Touch of The Master's Hand.

~Ken Brown, an adaptation of
Touch of the Master's Hand by Myra Brooks Welch

Table of Contents

Introduction

Does the title of this book, **Master in a Minute**, spark your curiosity? What is a **Master in a Minute**? Could you be a **Master in a Minute**?

What is a "master?" You might be a dog's master, or have an academic master's degree, or be a chess or bridge or golf master. Maybe you're a master of disguise! Here we are using the word *master* to refer to a skilled practitioner of art. Mastery, trust me, doesn't happen in a minute. It took me over thirty years of study and practice, practice, practice to draw the sunflowers here in this studio workbook. But, as the saying goes, life's best lived when we can *lean into* personal excellence. Each minute spent looking, studying, coloring, and creating in the Master in a Minute workbook inspires the joy of learning and wonder. That is a promise.

Sunflowers

The power of Creation is the ultimate Master in a Minute. Think about a sunflower. The power of Creation designed and grew sunflowers for so very many millions of years before a seed buried in the soil of my garden in Virginia blossomed into a ten-foot tall, thick-stemmed plant that produced magnificent wide flower heads, which I then drew in my workshop while snacking on roasted sunflower seeds.

In general, sunflower seeds are processed for cooking oil and the hulls and cake (what is left after the seeds are gone) are used in livestock feed. In traditional Native American culture, sunflowers were used for practical purposes in bread, as medical creams, as a dye and for body painting, and the root was made into a poultice applied to rattlesnake bites! Sunflowers were incorporated in their ceremonies and rituals to bring good luck and to ward off evil spirits.

Today, the sunflower is a symbol of Ukraine, which is known for its production of sunflower oil. During the Ukrainian-Russian war, a video showed a Russian soldier being confronted by a Ukrainian woman, who told him to "take these seeds and put them in your pockets so at least sunflowers will grow when you all lie down here."[1] The sunflower has thus become a symbol around the world of resistance, unity, and hope. [2]

Young sunflowers (but not fully grown ones) do indeed follow the sun from east to west throughout the day, known as heliotropic motion. This is a circadian rhythm that is regulated by the sunflower's response to blue light coming from the sun. We are going to be talking a lot about light in the Master in a Minute series—light that is vitally important to the growth of living things, the light and shadow of the artistic realm, and the light that is the energetic force of spiritual awakening within.

To the Incas, sunflowers were a symbol of the Sun. To Christians, they are related to the divine light of God since they look like the sun, and they are mentioned in Bible verses as symbols of beauty, faith, trust, and growth. In some Eastern religions, like Buddhism, sunflowers represent the human desire to turn towards the light, called the quest for en*light*enment. Just as sunflowers turn their faces towards the sun, we can turn to the light of the divine and trust in our spiritual growth.

The creative force of the universe is the supreme master designer. The same creative force that designed the sunflower also designed our eyes to see its beauty and my desire to share it with you. Unlike the images in computer-generated coloring books, my original drawings and paintings comprise the Master in a Minute® series—in other words, living art populates this book. Here, you are sharing my minute-by-minute experience of the Master of Creation. As always, I hope that my work inspires your soul and reminds you to seek out the light in your life.

---

[1] "Ukrainian woman offers seeds to Russian soldiers so 'sunflowers grow when they die' – video". *The Guardian*. (25 February 2022)

[2] Hassan, Jennifer, *The Washington Post* (2 March 2022), "The sunflower, Ukraine's national flower, is becoming a global symbol of solidarity"

How to use this book

Does the image resonate inside you? Color the sunflowers to reflect your own positivity and joy, loyalty and devotion, growth and resilience, all attributes assigned to sunflowers.

As you channel your inner artist, relax. I wonder if a doing a short meditation on a drawing, before beginning to color, would be transformative? I'll be honest, I drew these puppies to share the hypnosis I experienced when surrendering, over and over again, to the Mystery of the sunflower's Cosmic Geometry. No matter what, as you come face-to-face with the beaming sunflowers, enjoy your journey. Let your heart, mind, and soul color your experience. In a bright shining mood, the sunflowers may be a golden yellow. In a more contemplative state of mind, the sunflowers may reflect a quiet blue of your inner sky. So, free your imagination, and bring your personality and spirit to the flowers I drew.

My drawings are now always your friends.

May you find coloring brings you pure simple joy.

And may your encounter with sunflowers bring love of self.

Jennet Inglis™

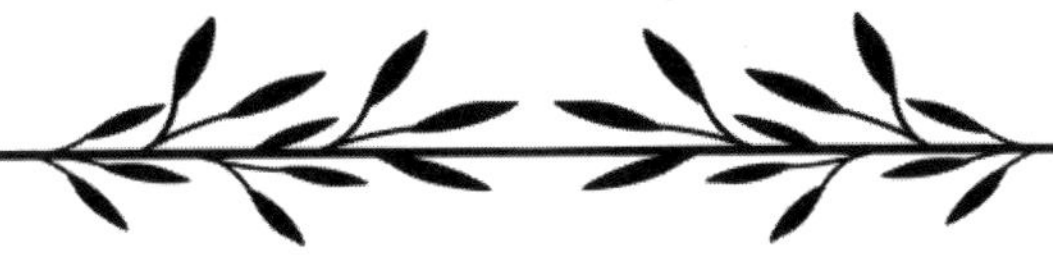

Getting Started

- Enjoy the images and reflect on the art. Spark your creativity!
- Color in the sunflowers and their details. Extra blank pages are included. Cut or tear them out and use them behind your drawings to prevent "spotting."
- Sketch, collage, or write on the blank leaf-framed pages.
- Study the design concepts in the Mind Treasure pages.
- Share your discoveries with friends at https://masterinaminute.com
- Ask the artist questions on https://masterinaminute.com

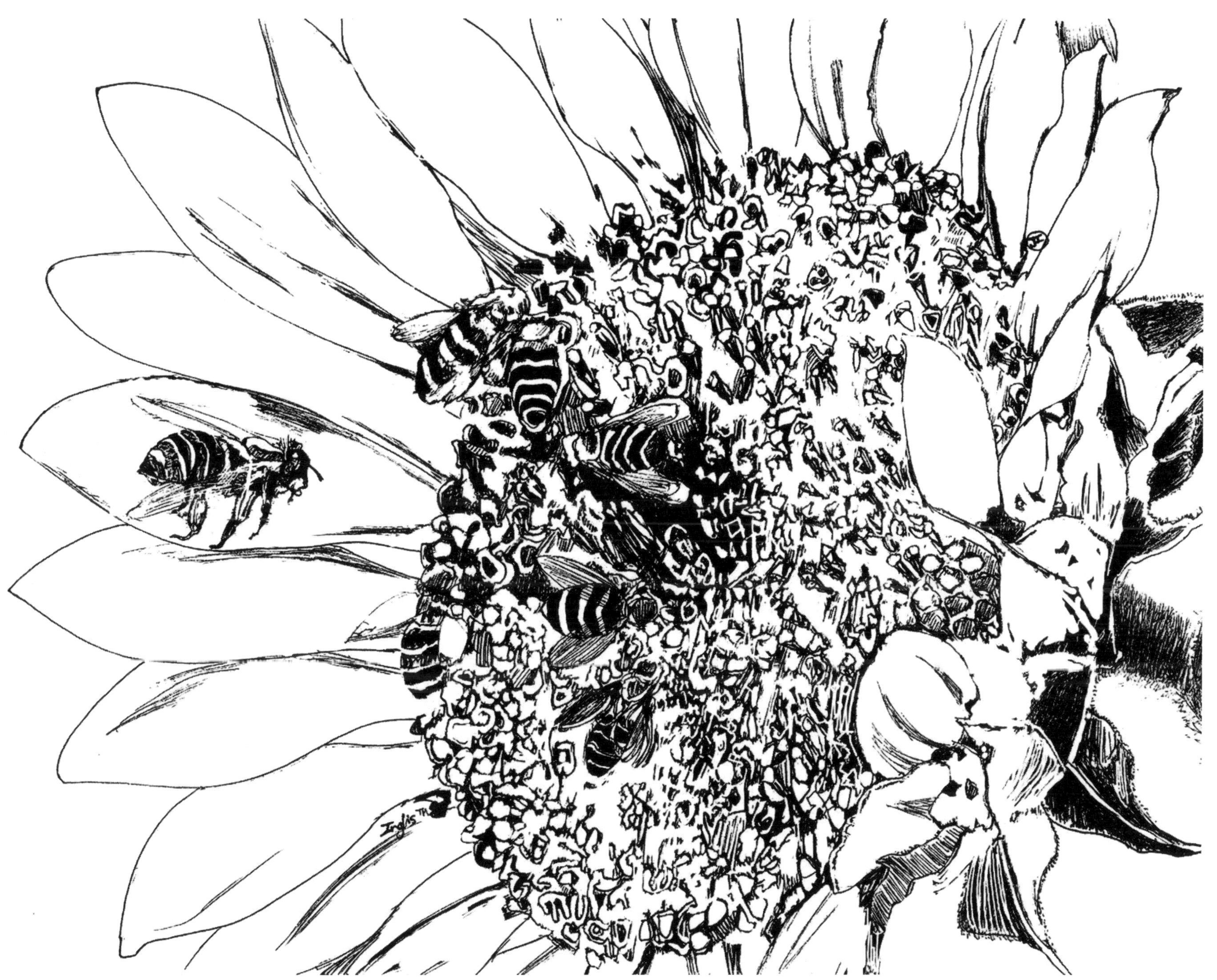

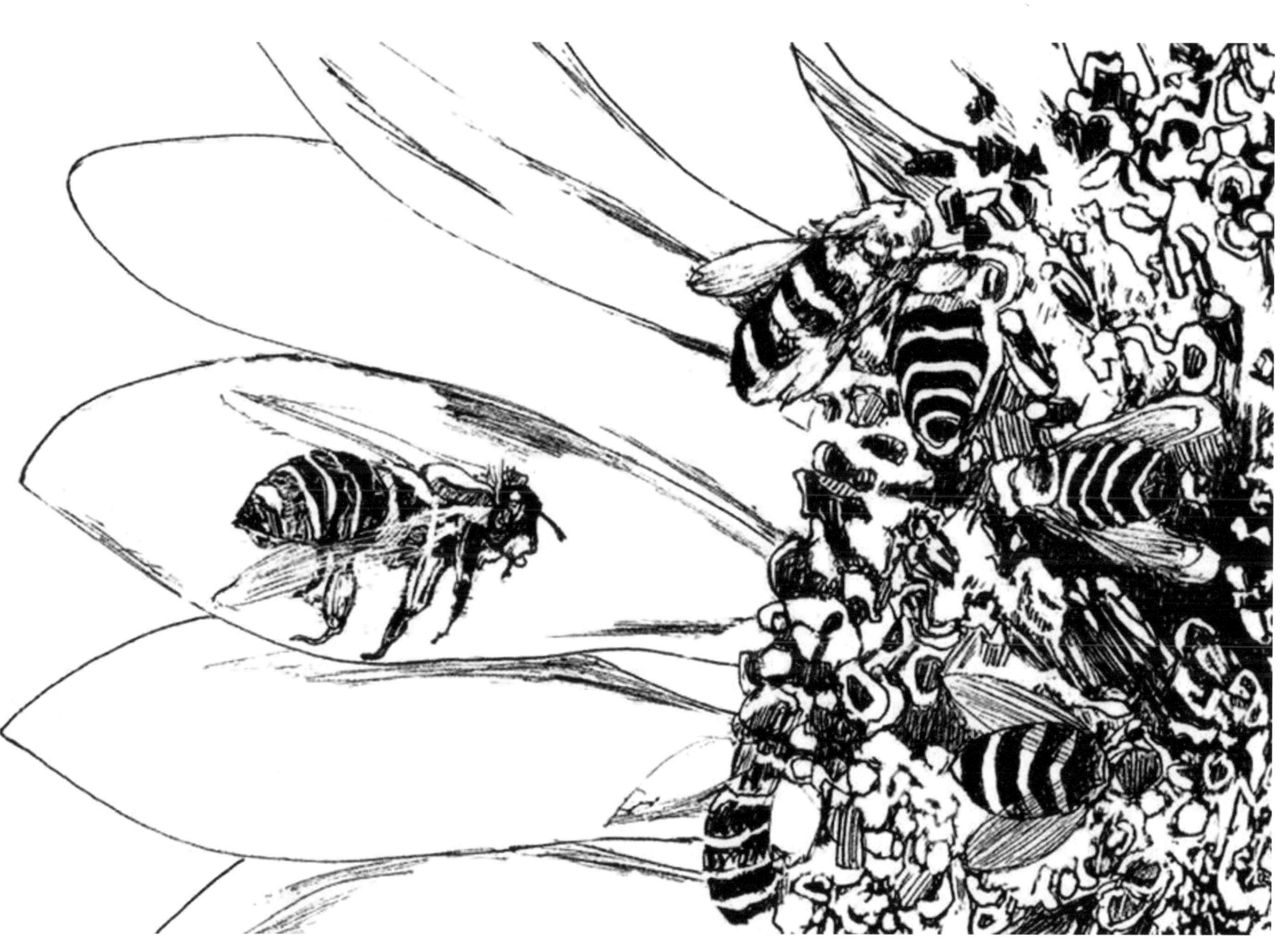

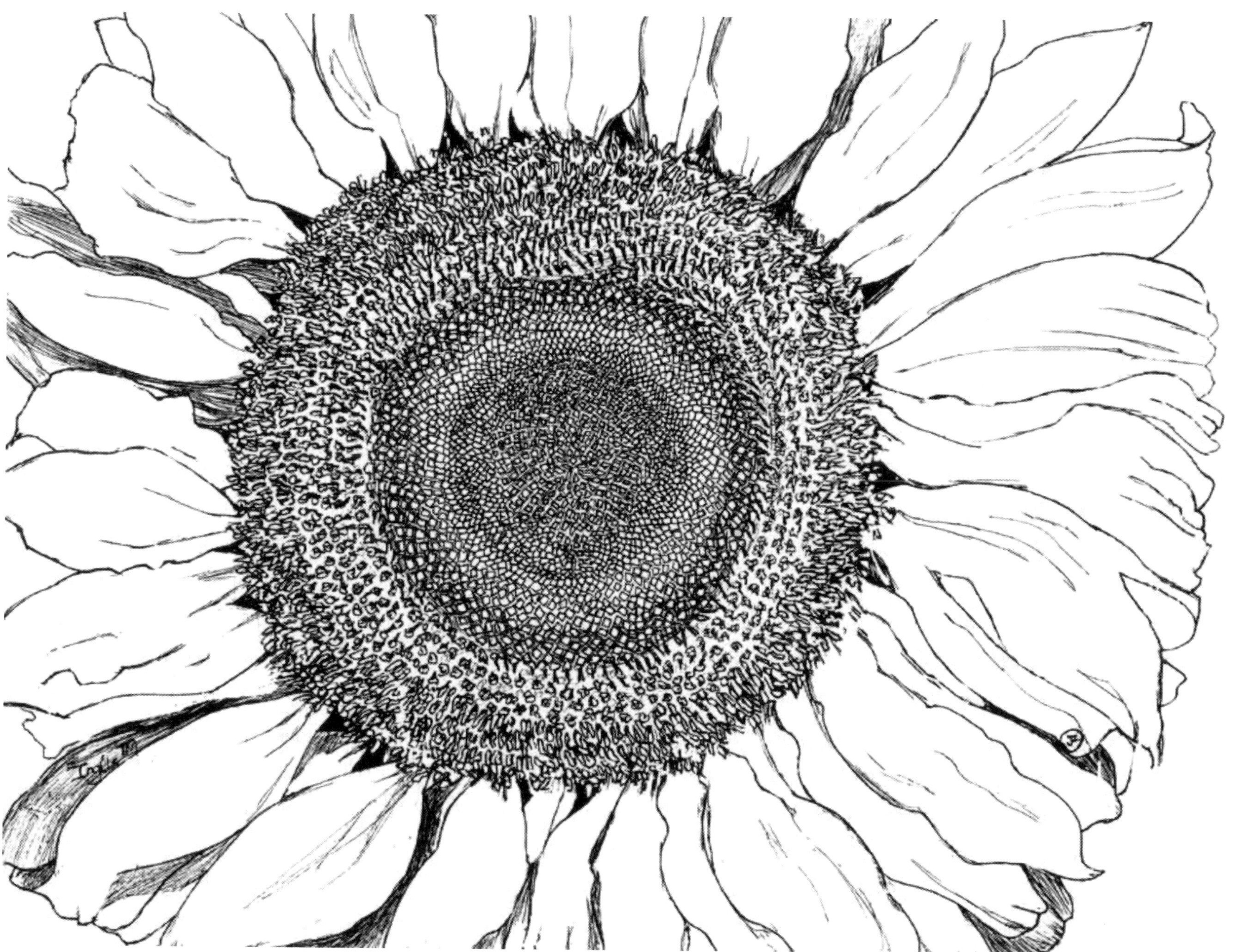

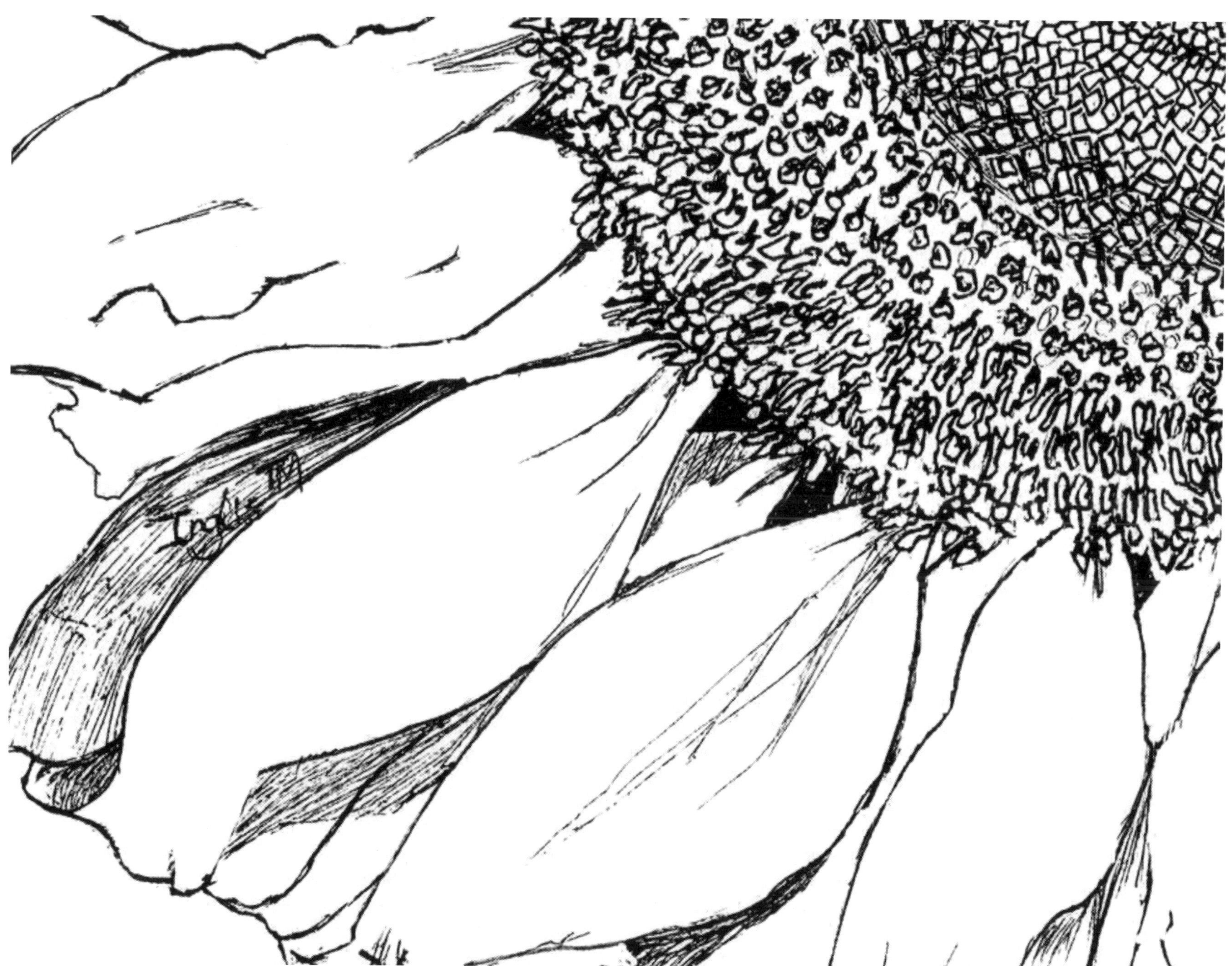

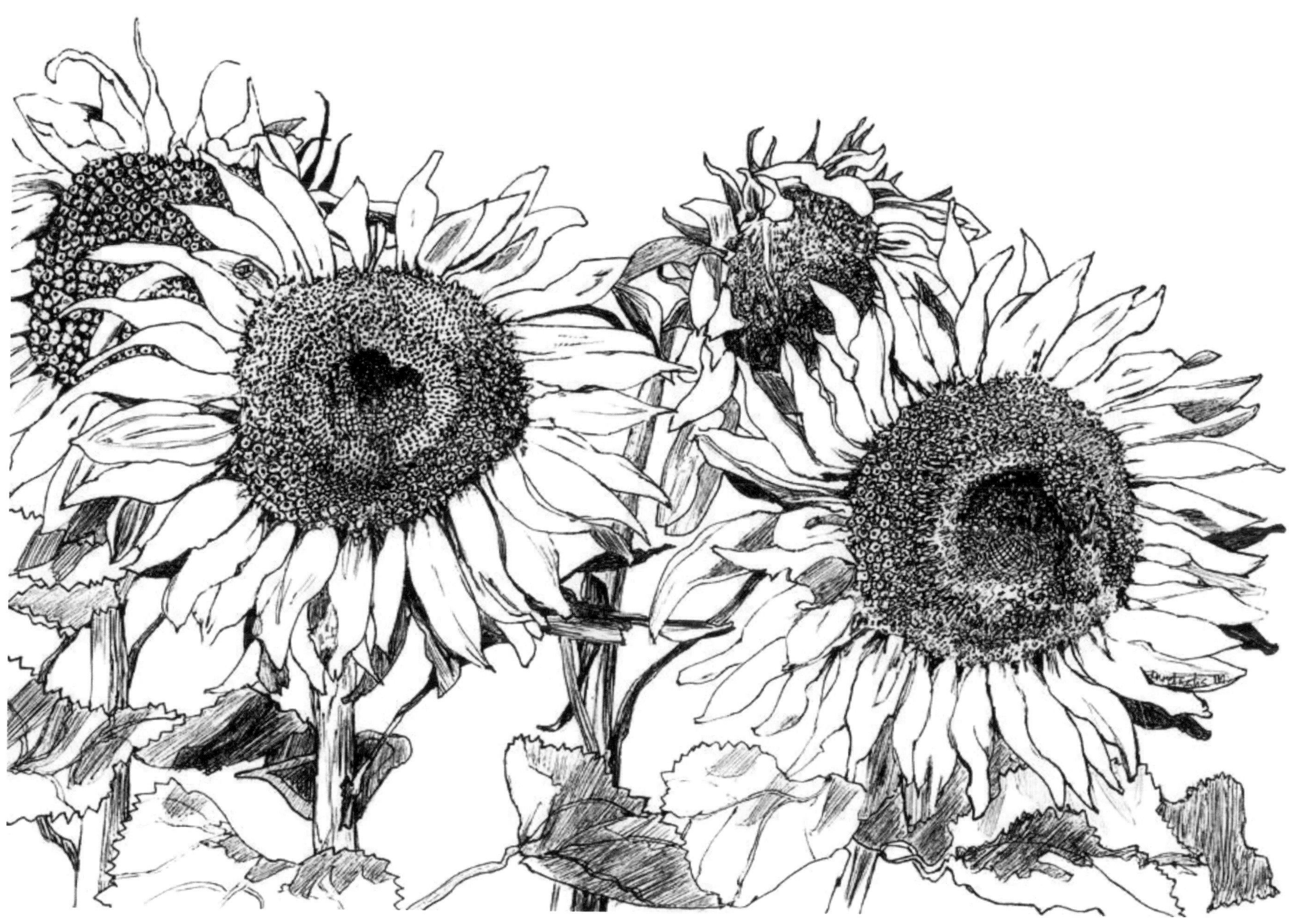

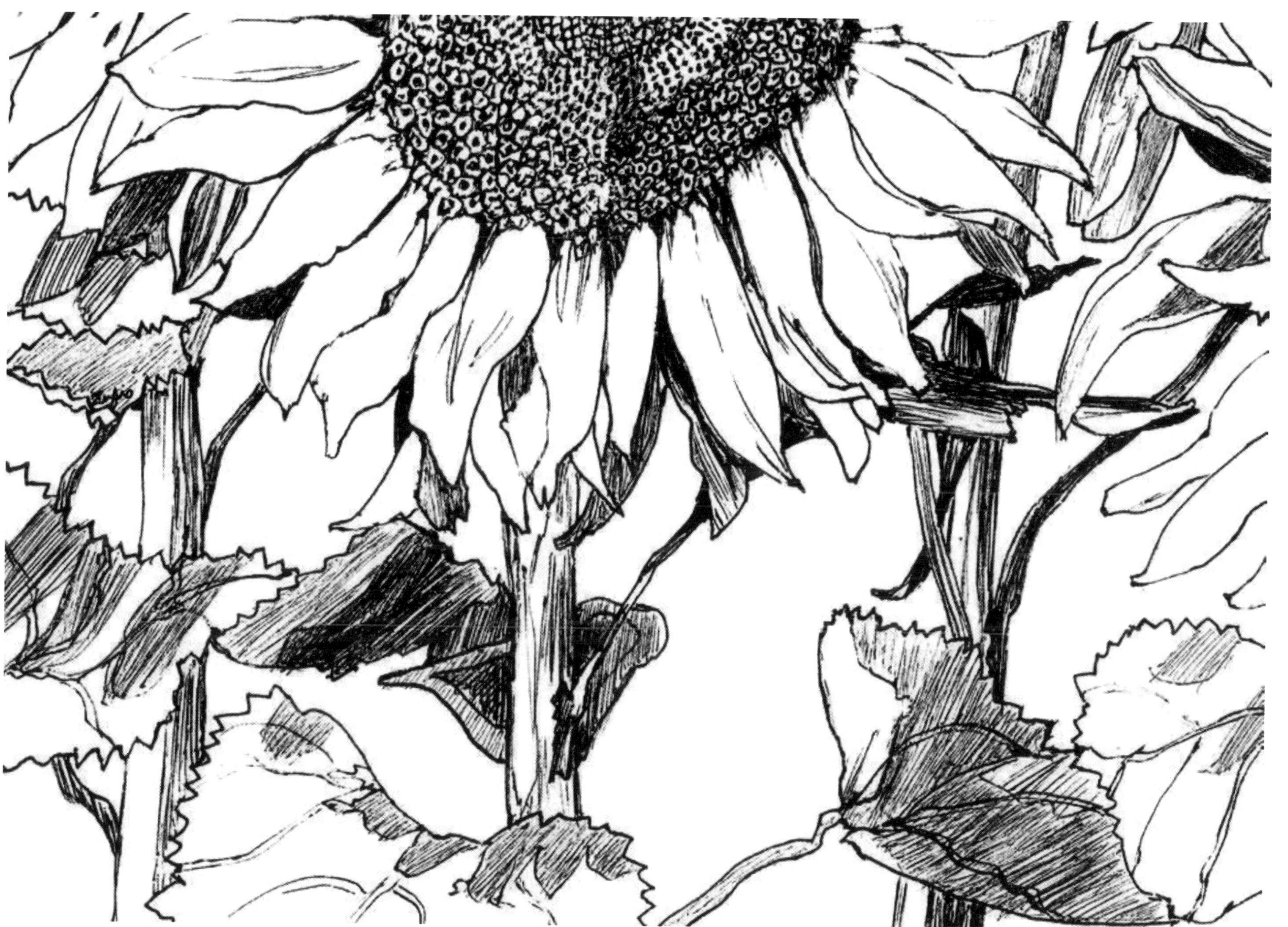

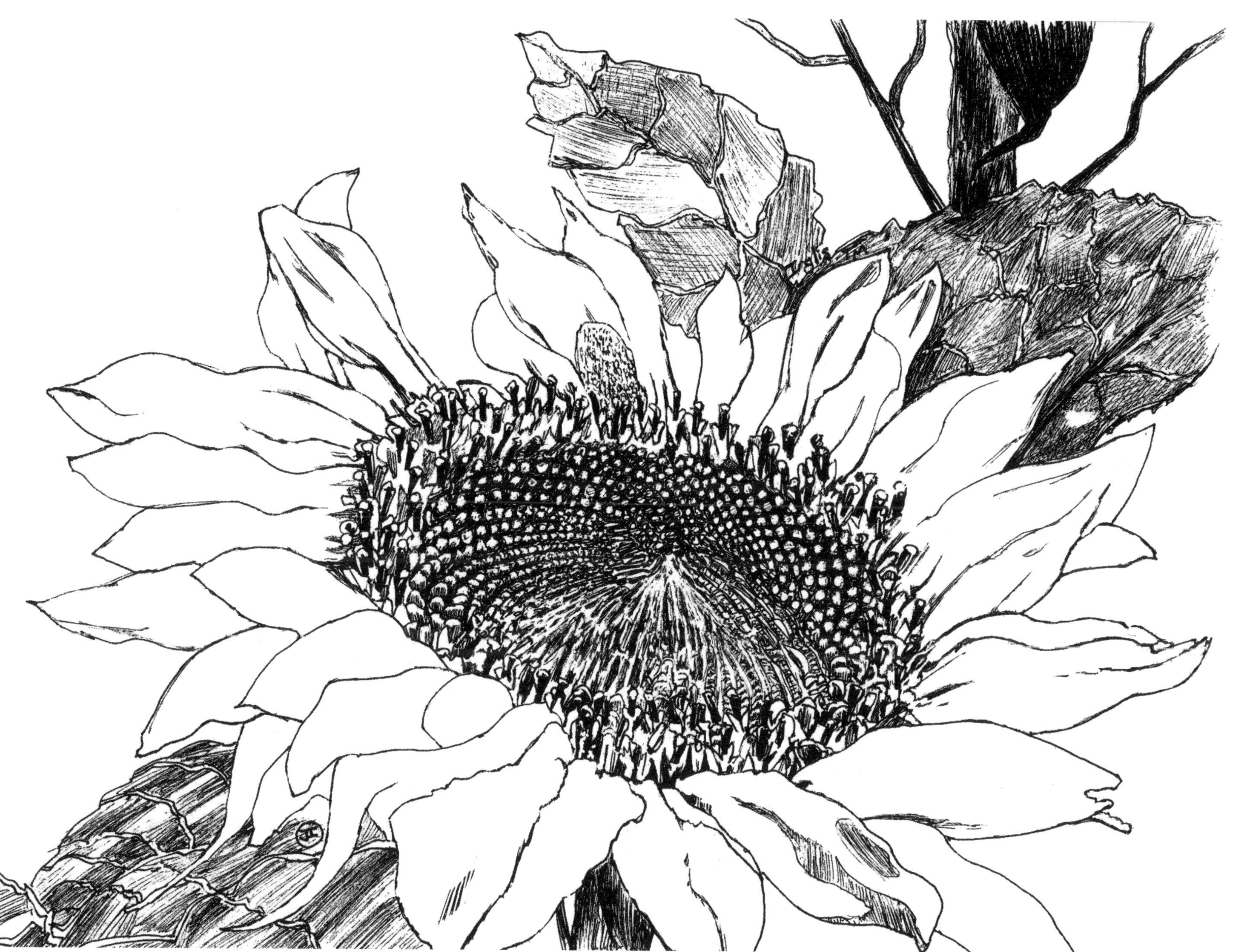

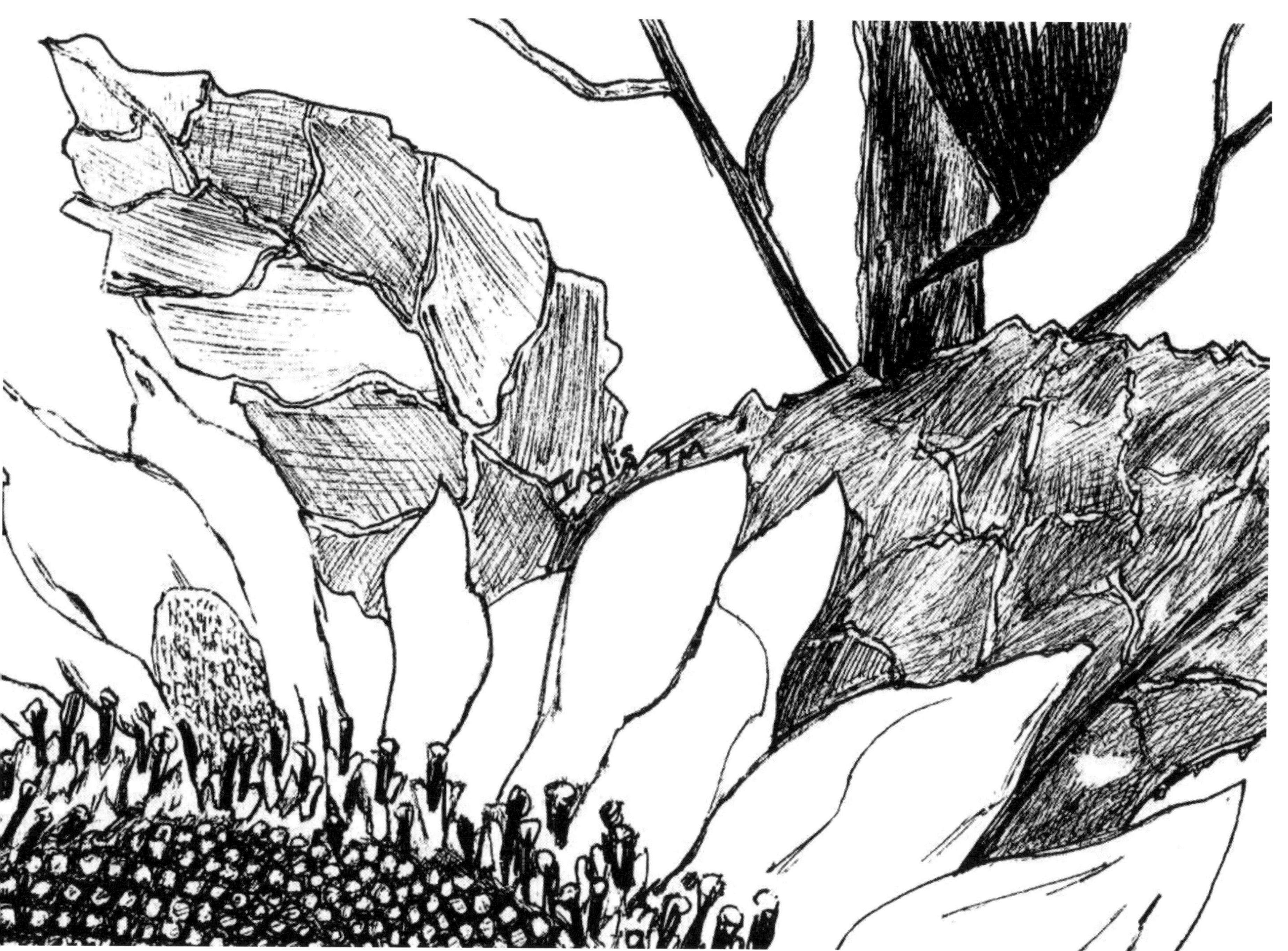

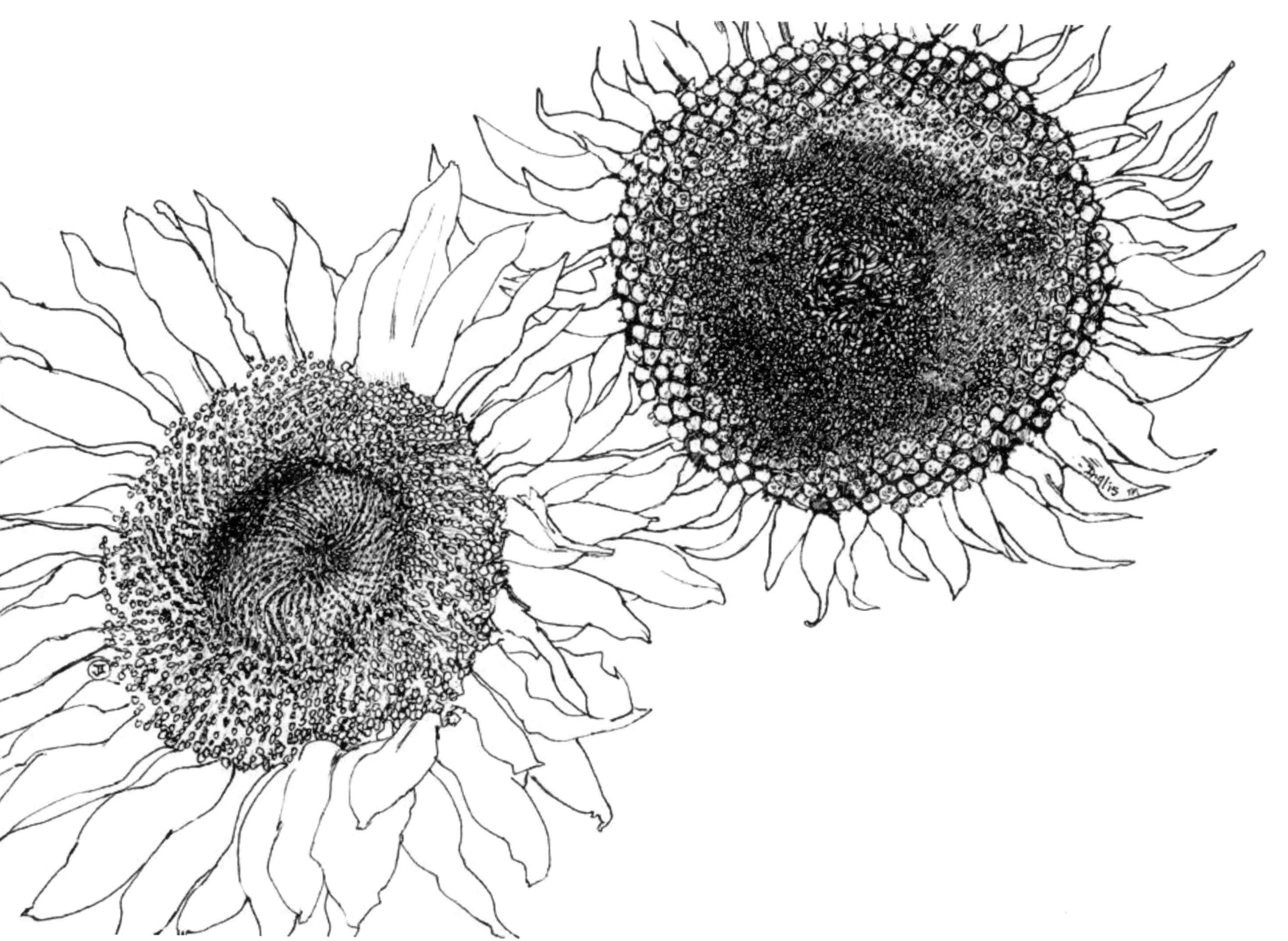

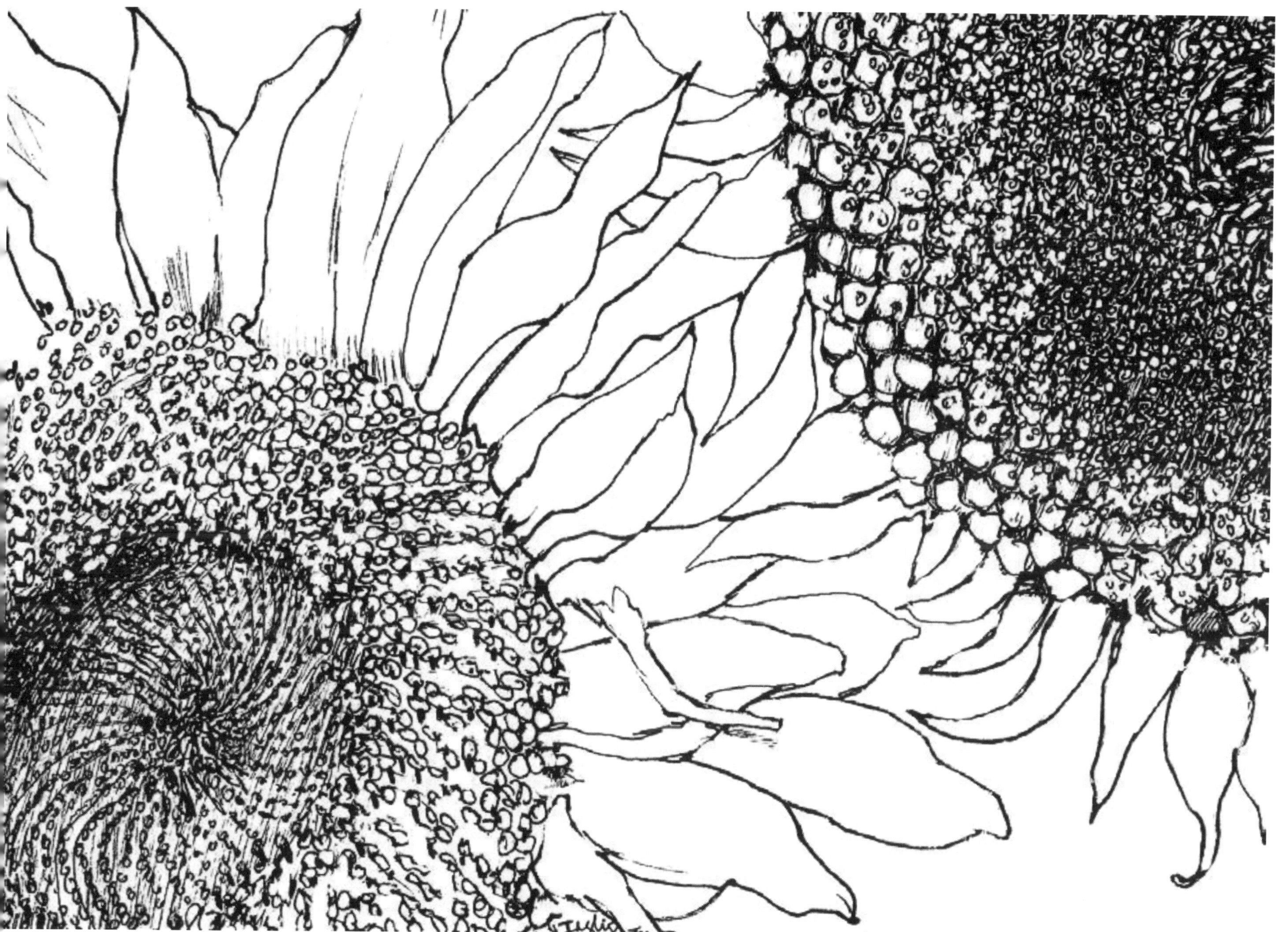

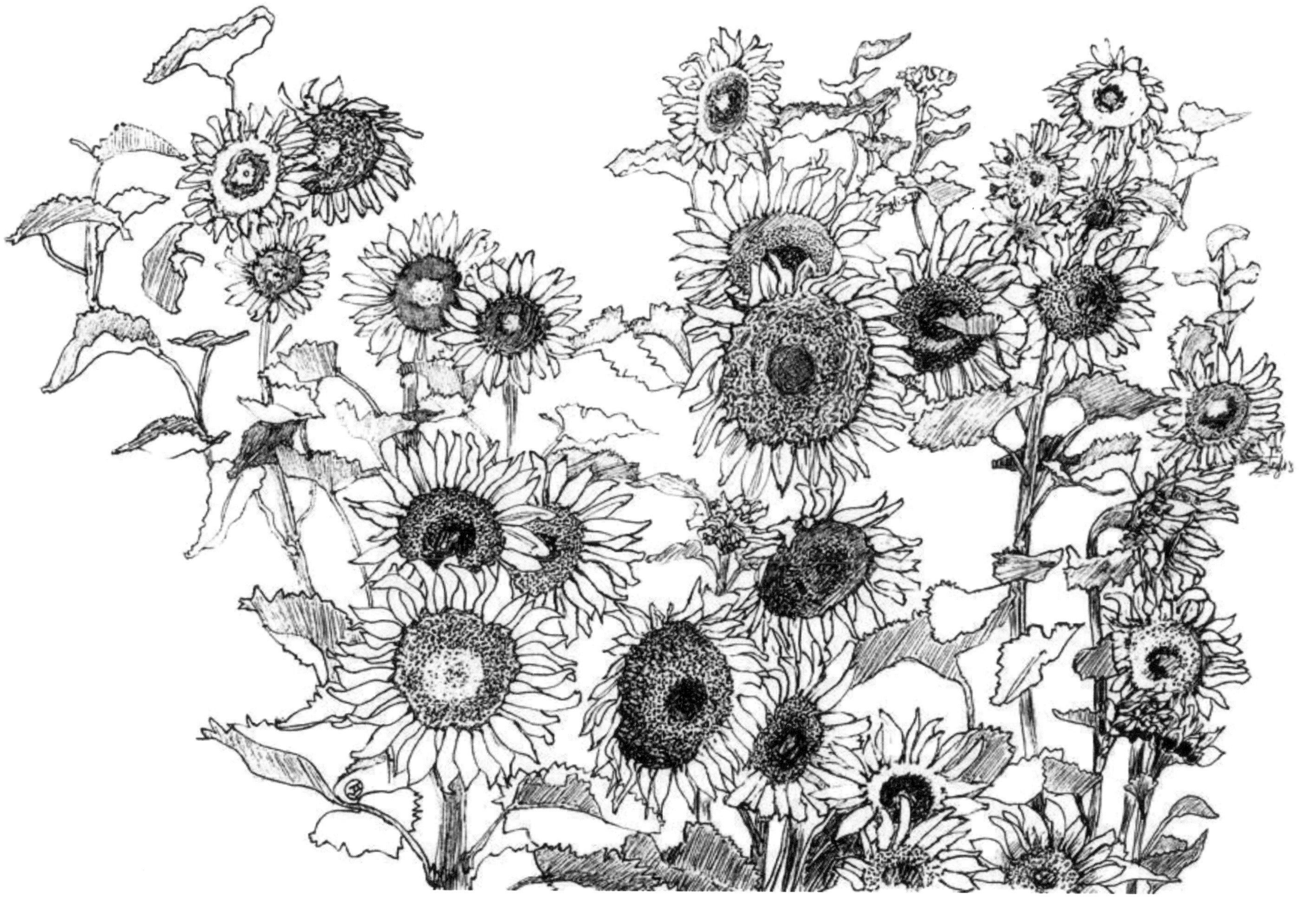

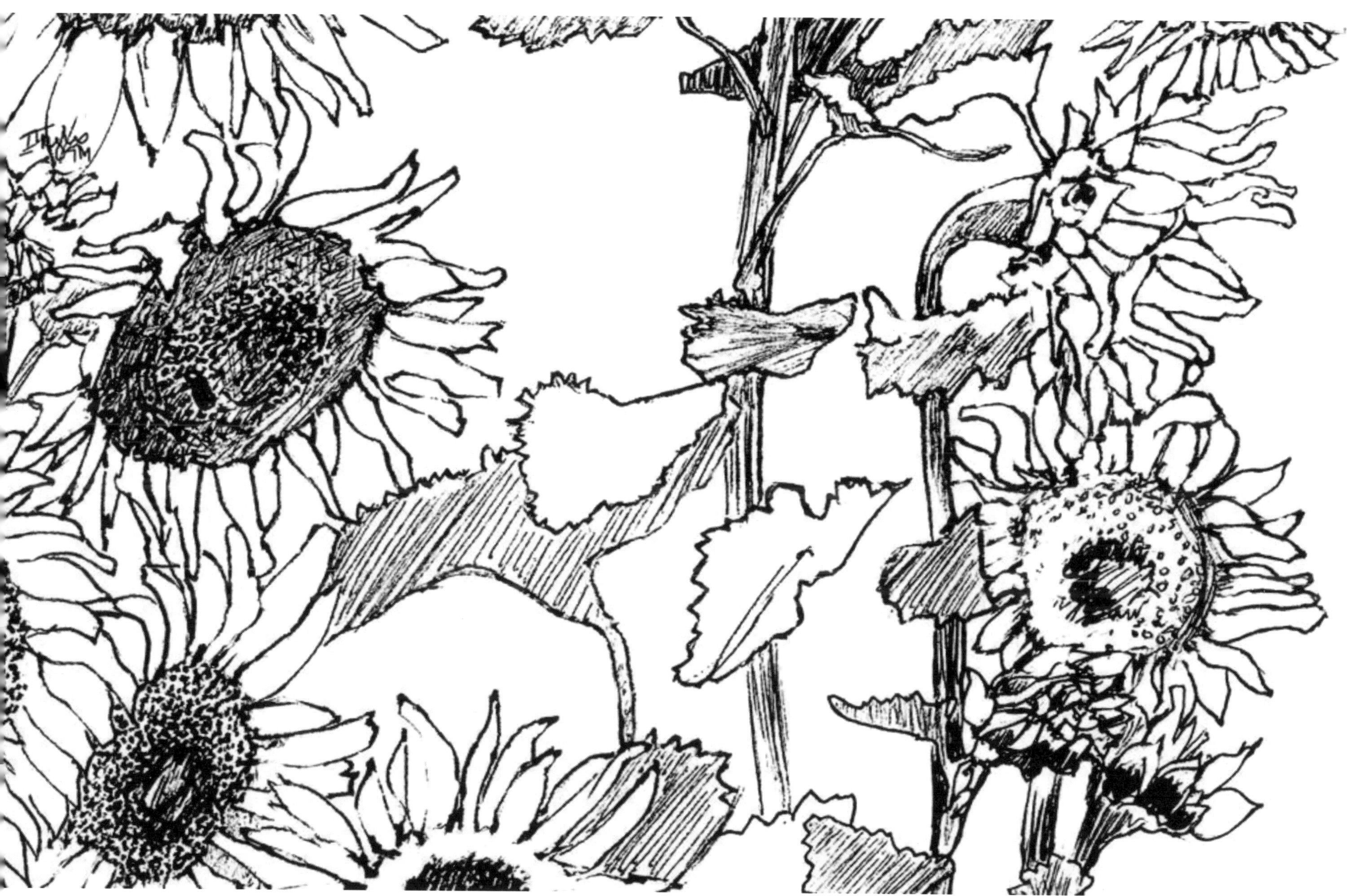

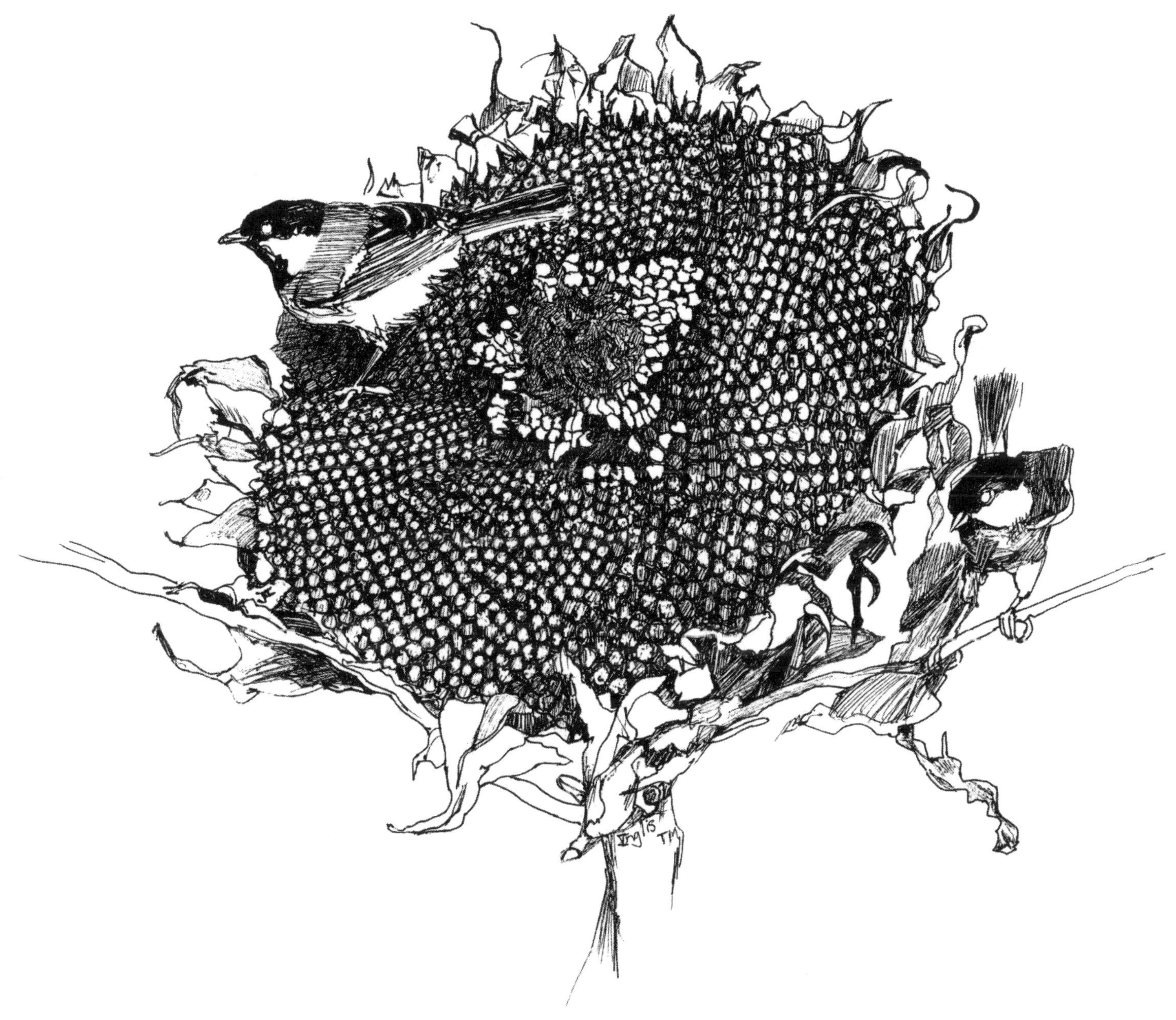

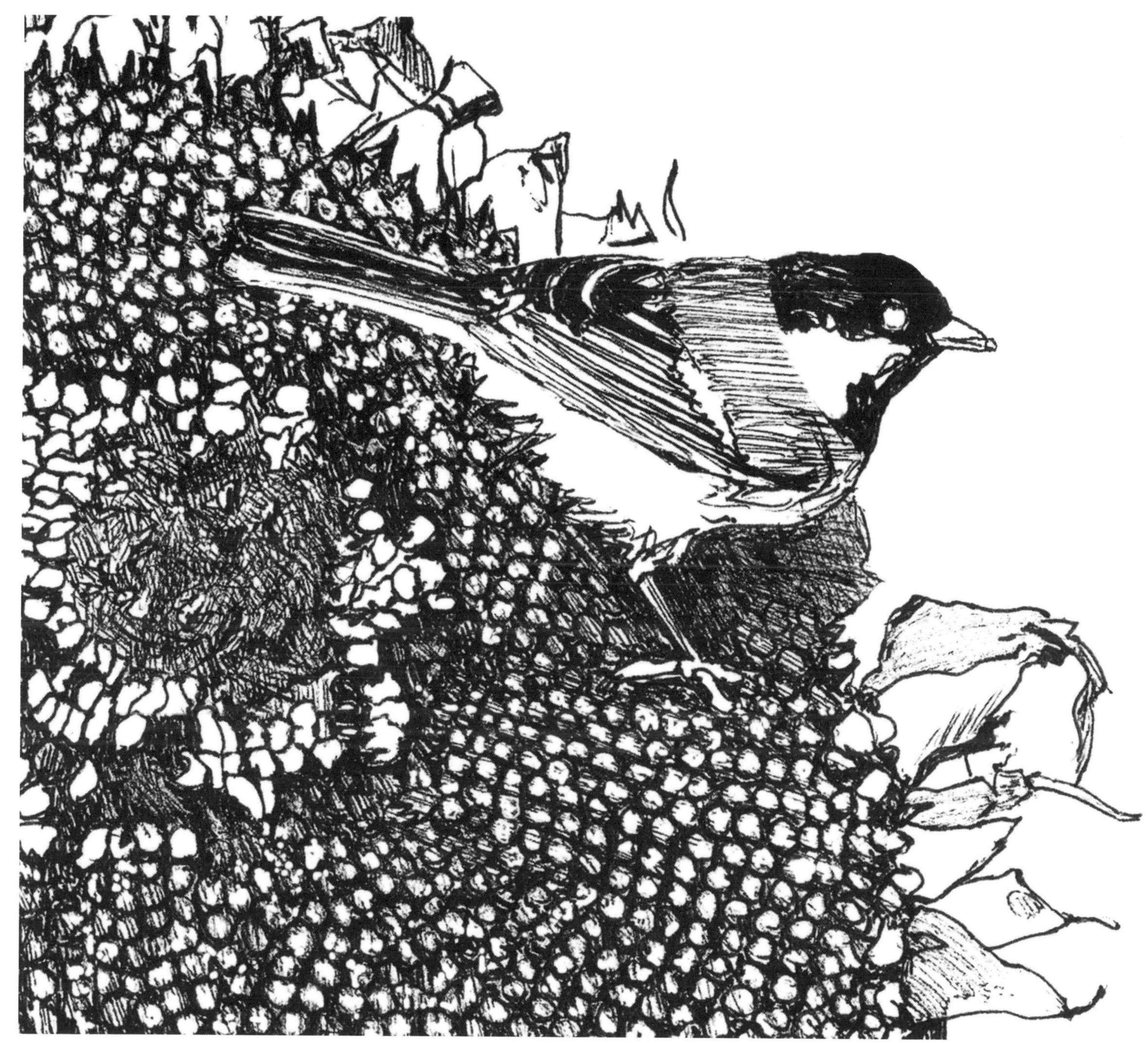

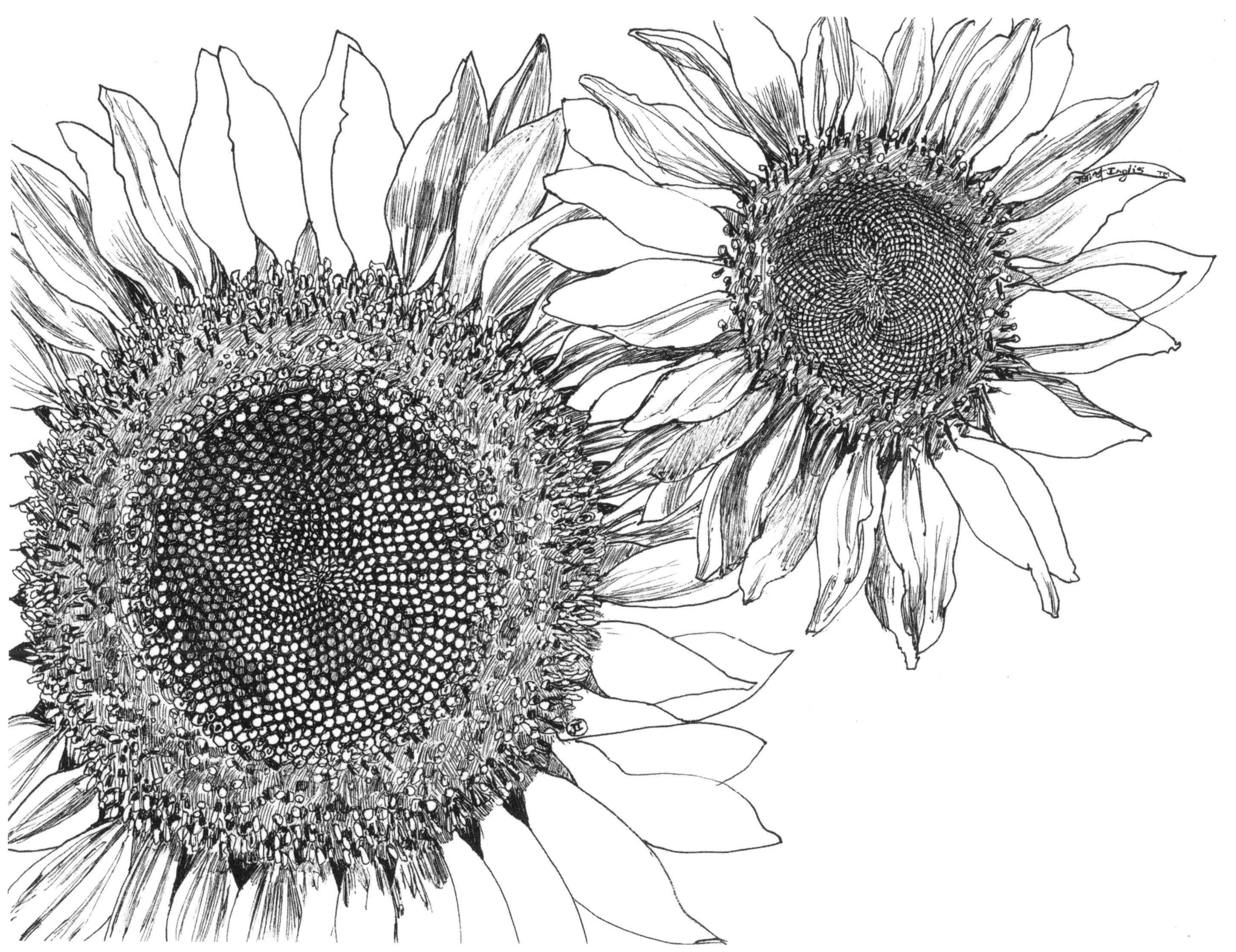

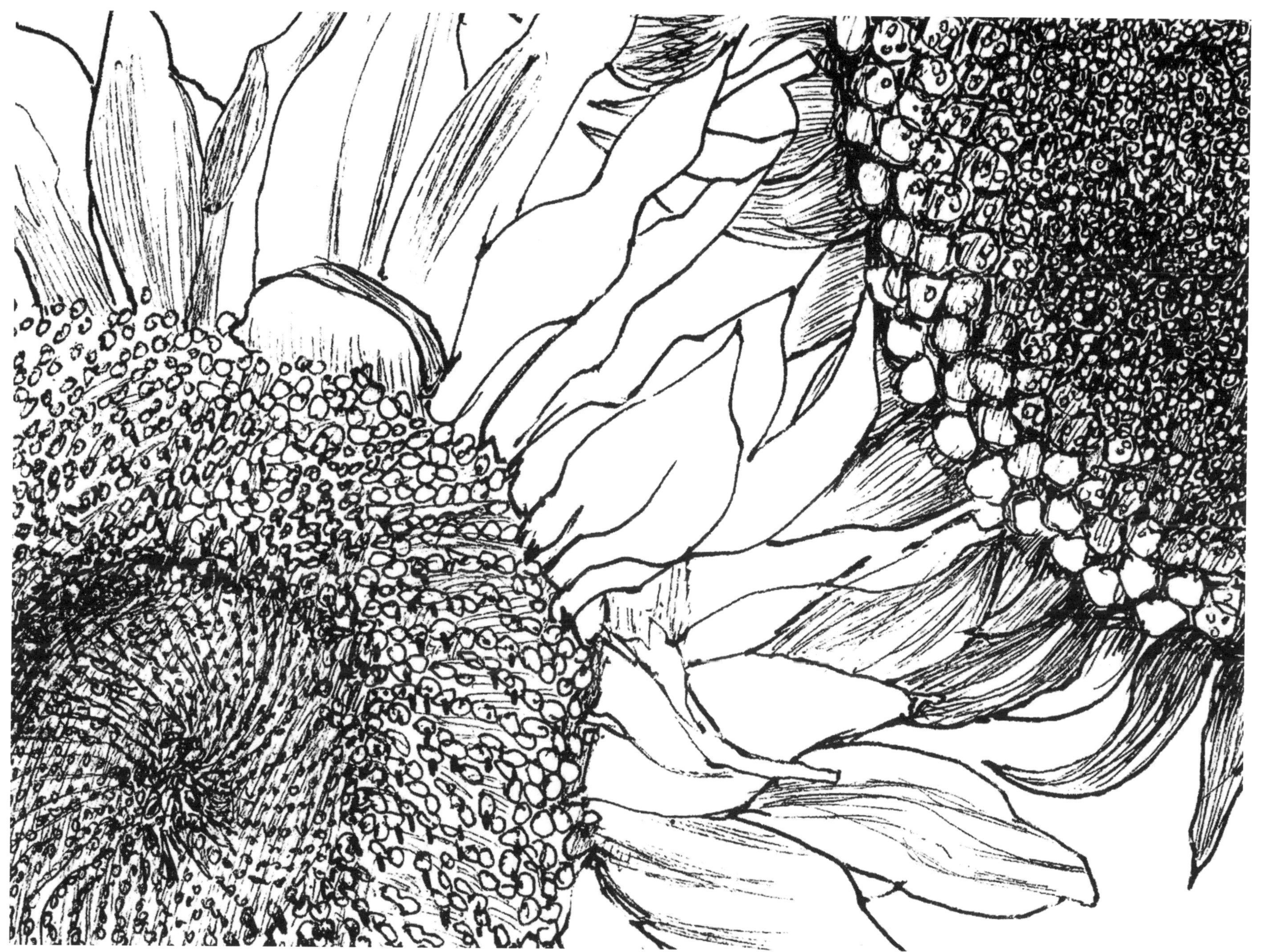

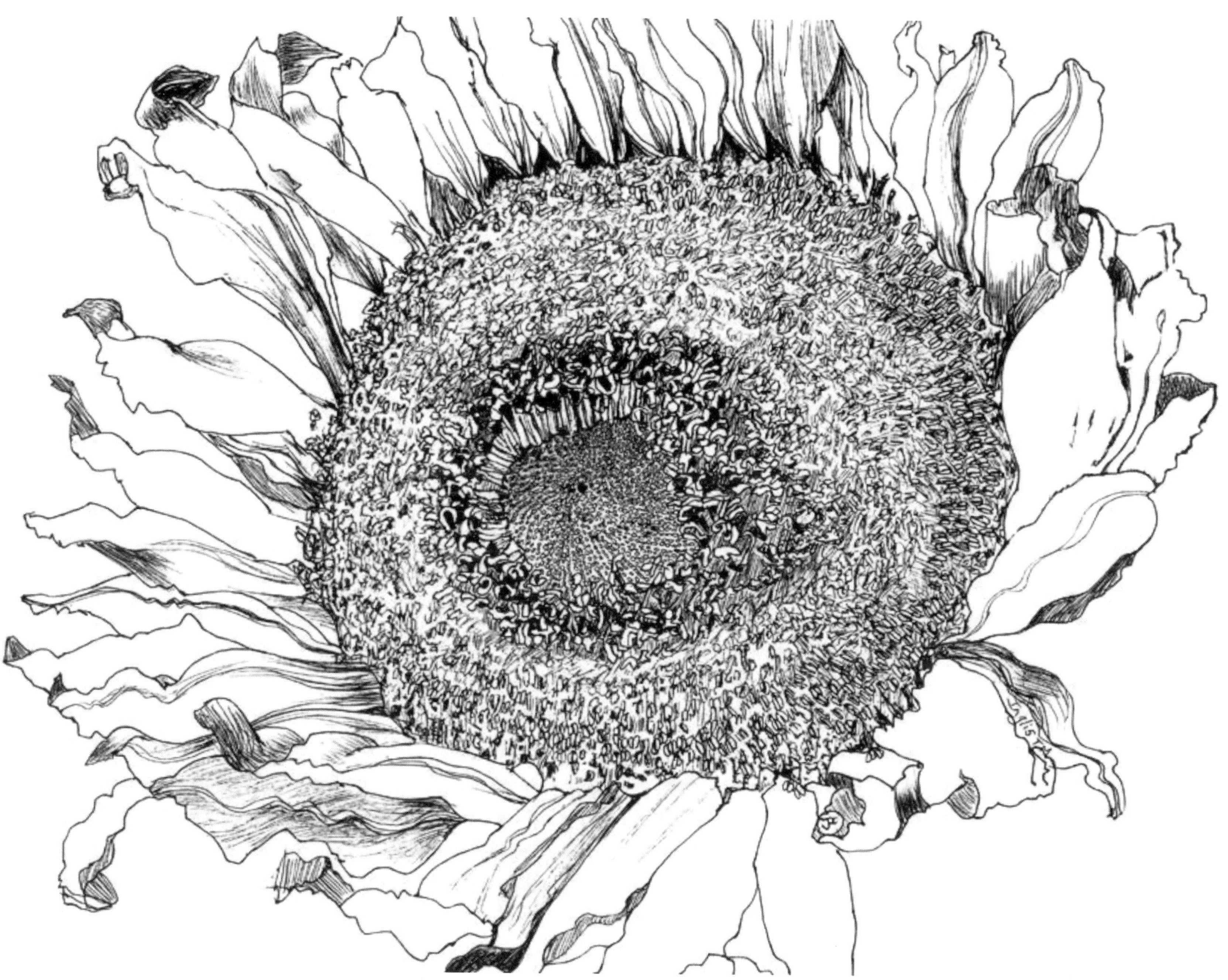

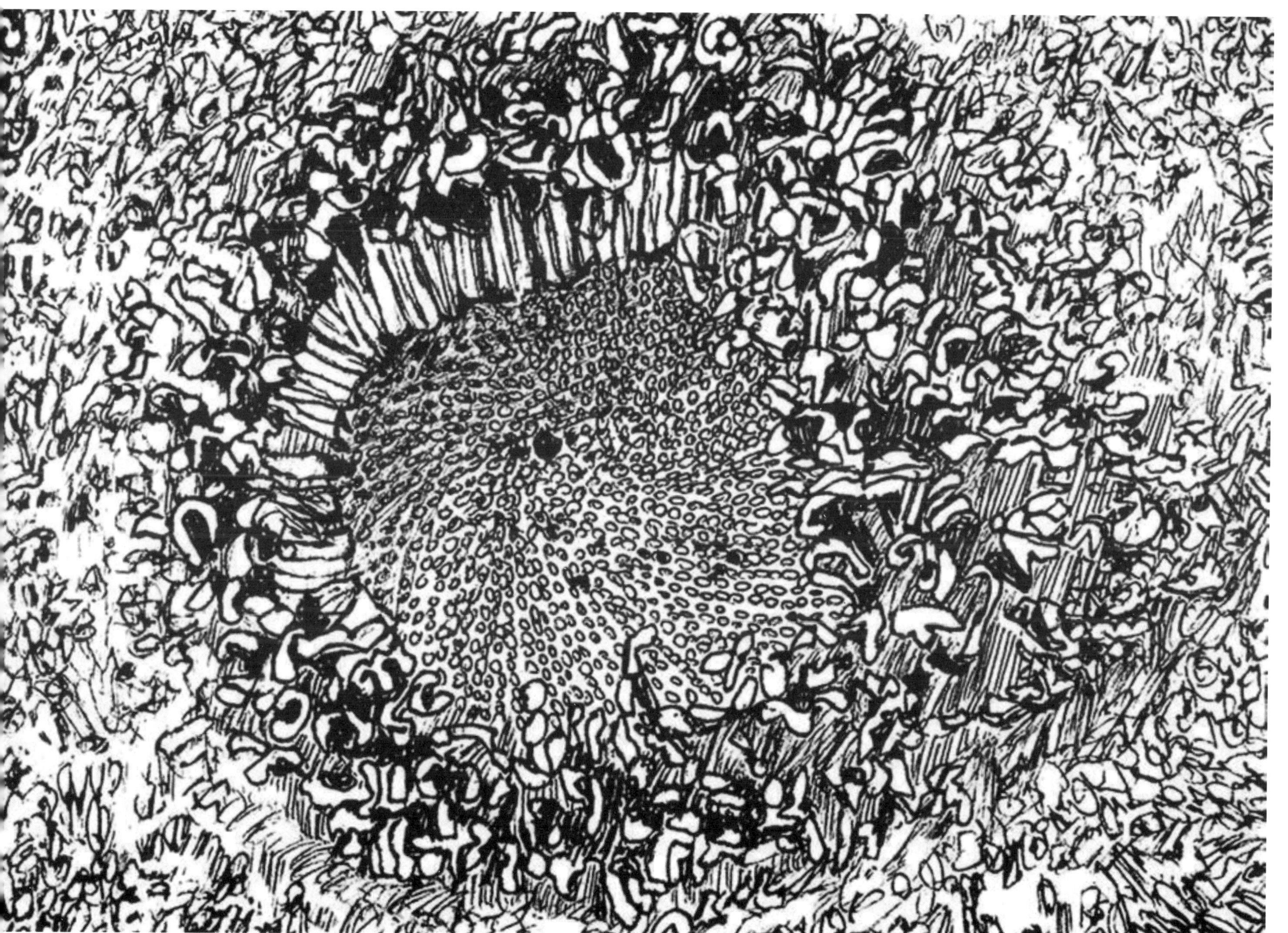

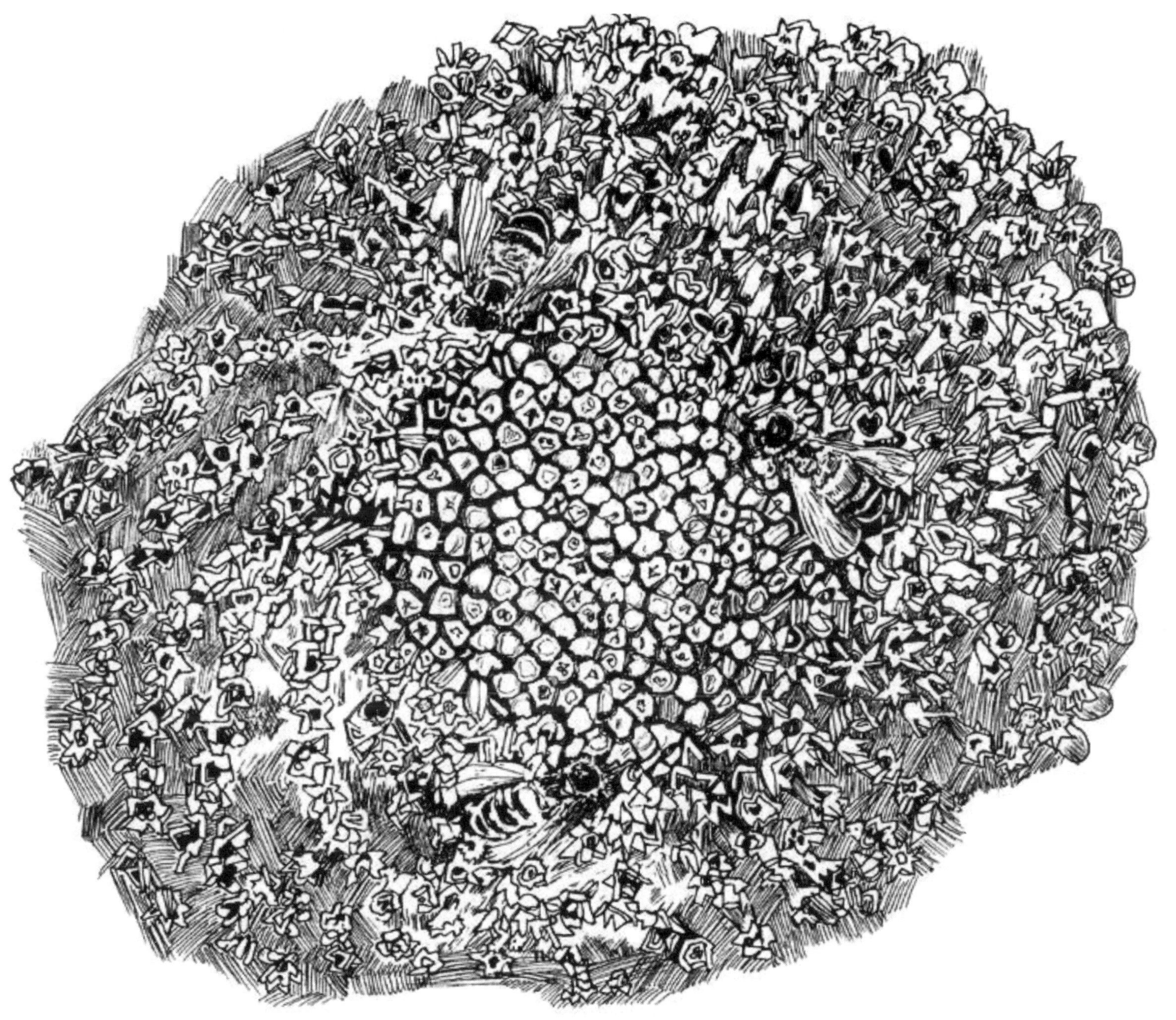

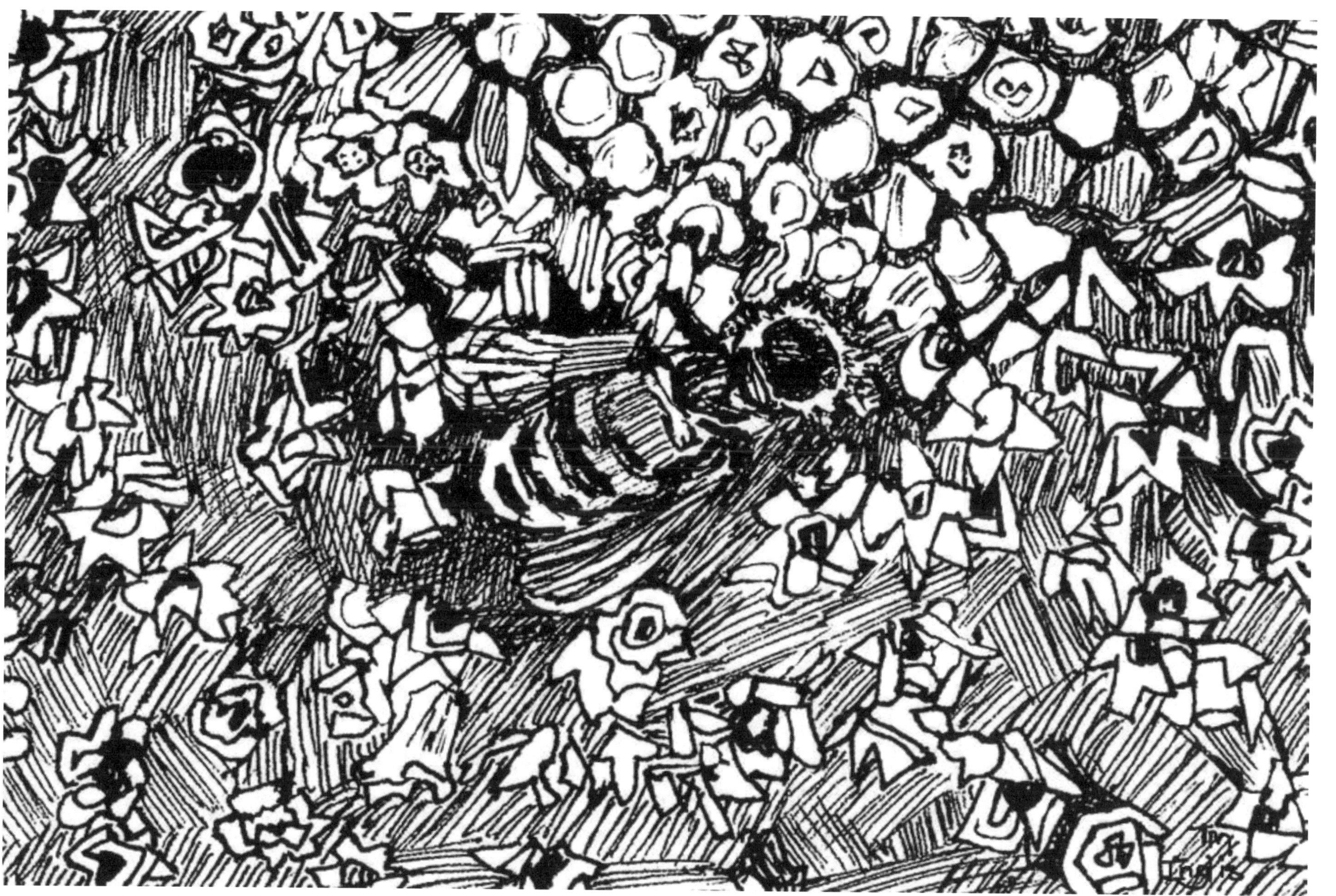

Fifteen Mind Treasures

The CENTER

Return to Mother Nature's first principle of beauty—strong living centers. A unifying focus, like a nucleus, gives life to the whole. An animated, vital, positive living center can be supported by other smaller strong centers. A strong living center is a magnet for the natural rhythmic movement of the human eye. The primary universal pattern of motion for the human eye roams around a figure eight, with our eyes always returning to the center. Keep in mind, this figure-eight pattern is horizontal, lying down on its side, like the sign for infinity.

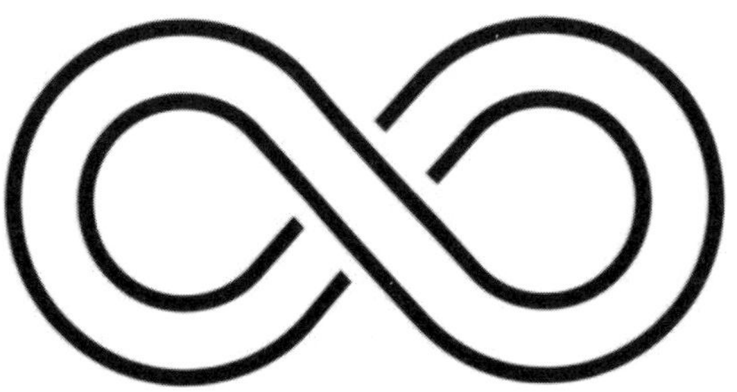

Quiet, Hidden, Powerfully Integrative Center

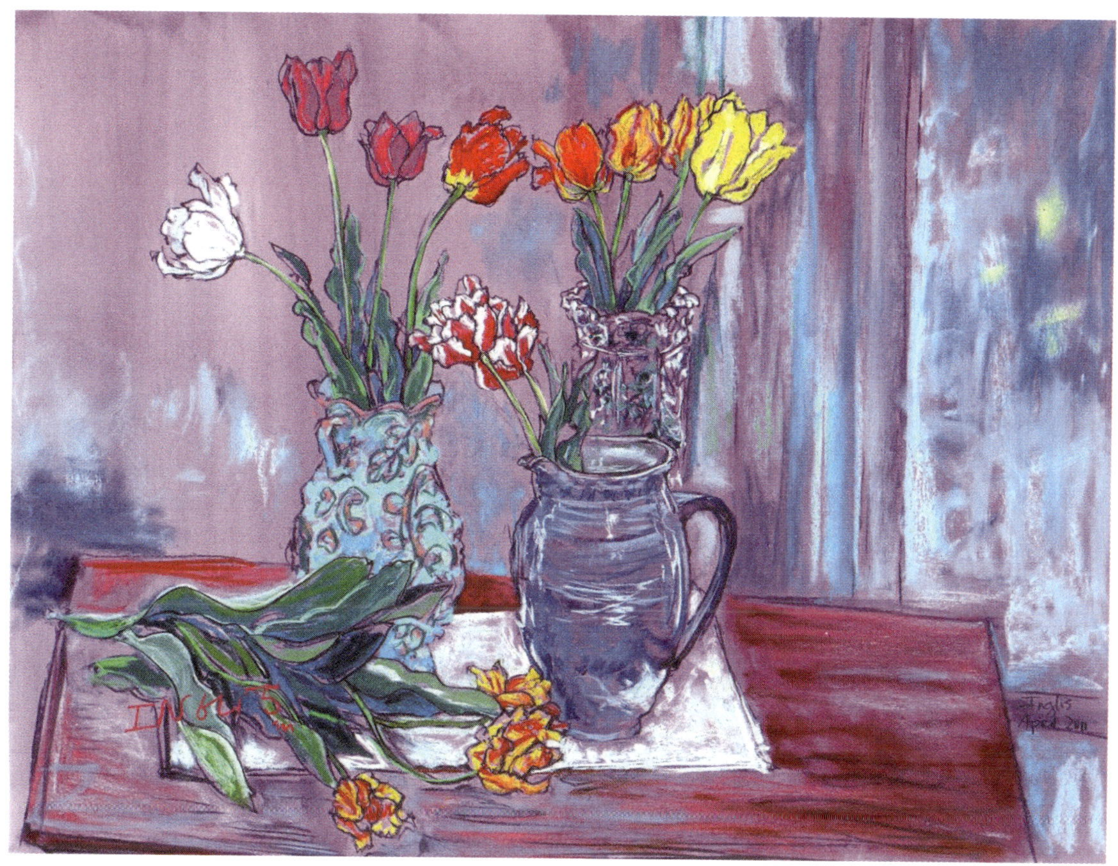

"Spring Tulips"

The center is all about the strength of the red-and-white tulip: are they about to fall apart? Are they dying like the tulips laying on the table. Did the shriveling tulips come out of the blue vase? The very edge of the vase holding the tulips. Strong visual centers contain everything and nothing. The eyes, psyche, and heart love to return to a magnetic center. It's instinct at the most primal, and evolved, level. Life and death cycle and return, always, to the Center.

“Spring Tulips”
22x30 inches (55.8x76.2cm)
Oil pigment on paper

Grounded Center

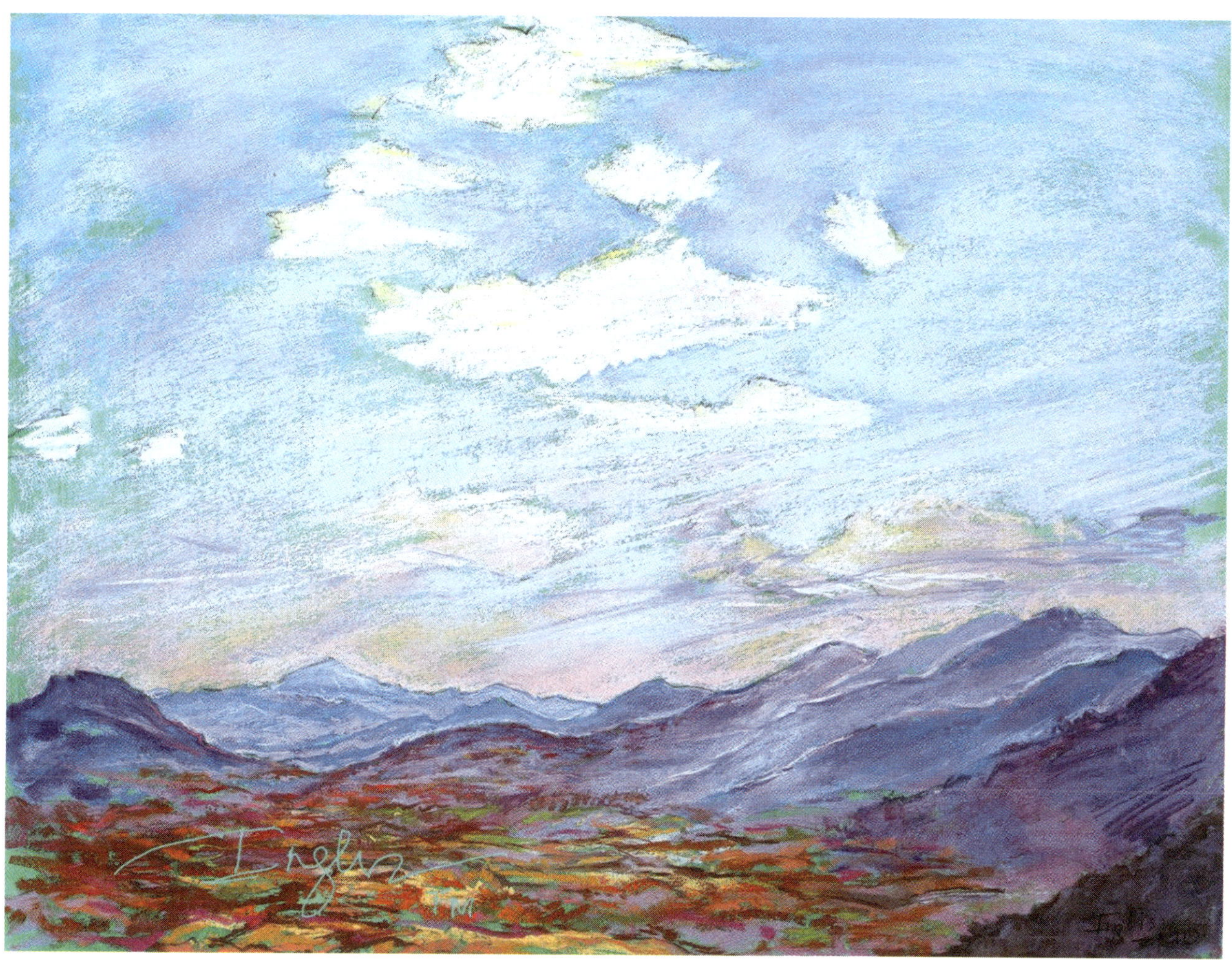

"December Haze over Rockfish Gap"

Foreshortening gives us a grounded center in a *unified field* between the far, far horizon and what would be at our feet. At the edge of the cliff, we venture back and forth, down into the valley, on to the horizon, and then back. The cloud formations center us in the composition, calling us to the horizon. And we journey home again . . . to our center.

“December Haze over Rockfish Gap”
18x24 inches (45.7x60.9cm)
Proprietary Dry Pigment Impasto (DPI) on paper

Etheric Center

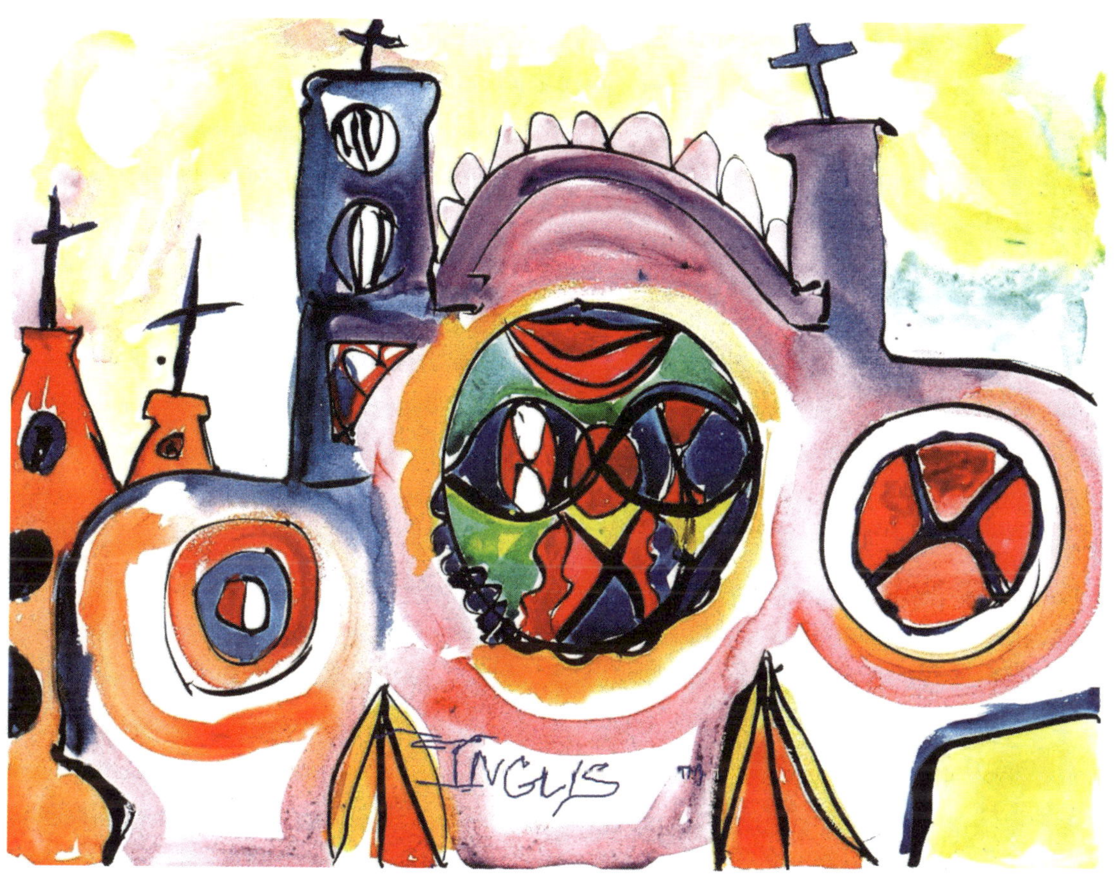

"Body Temple: Roseheart, 1"

This painting uses multiple smaller centers to support the primary center—the rose window. The "Body Temple" in us springs from the heart of the painting and spiritualizes our body and mind with light and color. We can all find our center of magic.

“Body Temple: Roseheart, 1”
22x30 inches (55.8x76.2cm)
India ink & watercolor on paper

Potent Texture

Beautiful powerful centers are supported by the use of potent texture. Handmade—natural, vulnerable, irregular, not measured or contrived. Forceful and independent of our machine world. The texture of authentic imaginative freedom. The feeling of the artist's abandon in creation. Connection to the grace and surrender in the moment of raw beauty: in the viewer and in the artist. Great wholeness and organic, definitely not perfect texture. Vulnerable beauty allowing potent life to emerge.

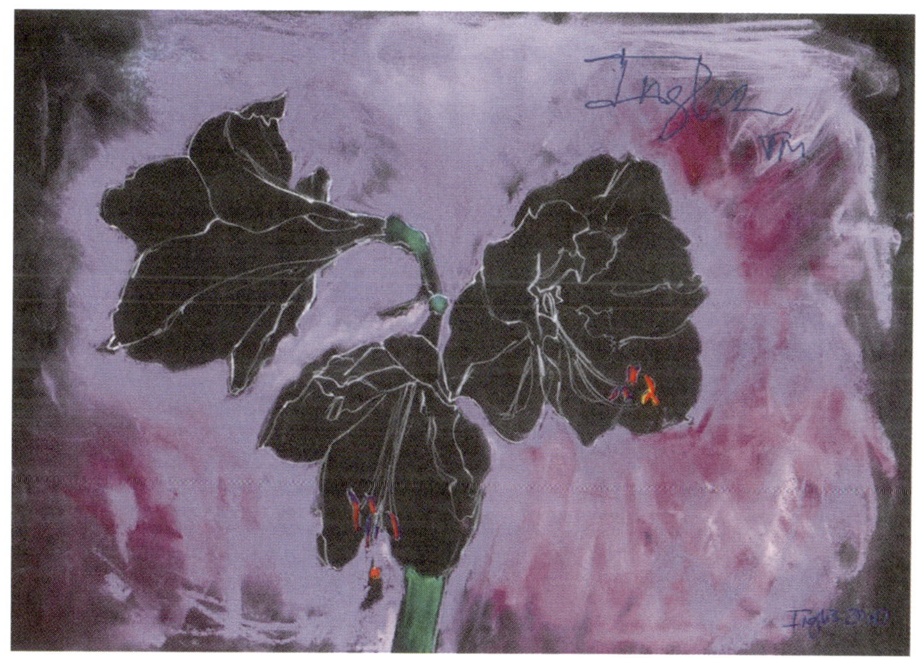

"Midnight Nimbus Amaryllis"

First, the texture of pure light suspends a core circle of essentially blank silhouettes. Meanwhile, our primal (ancient) impulse of recognition (memory) allows us to settle upon the void represented by the flowers. And then we realize that the space and light circling the flowers become mas

“Midnight Nimbus Amaryllis”
14x20 inches (35.6x50.8 cm)
Gouache, pencil, & pigment on museum rag board

Timeless Texture

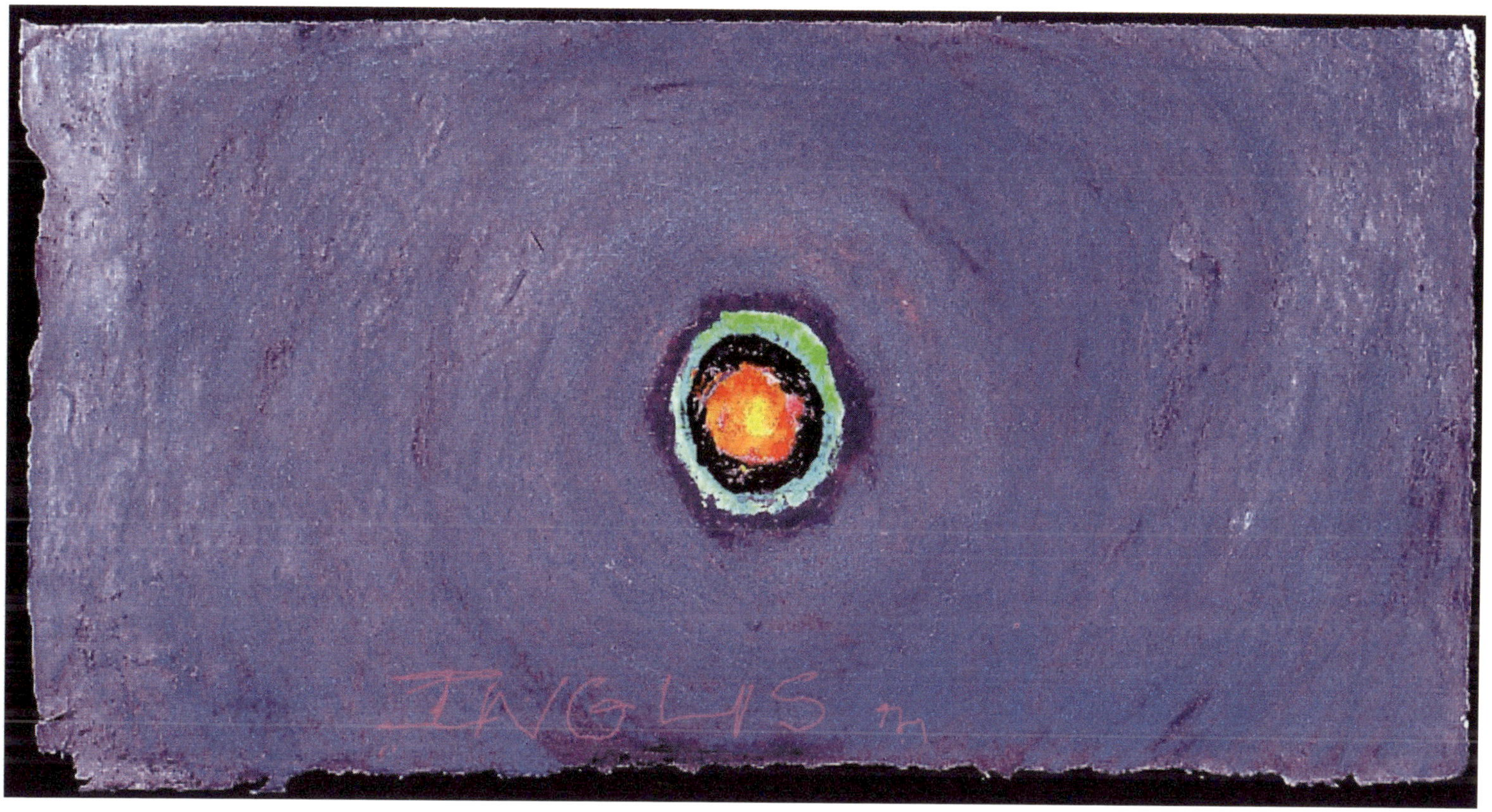

"Pulsar Baby"

In this painting, texture is a "force of friction" upon your eye. It slows you down so that you lose yourself in the surrounding and supporting of the center, our baby star. Fresh and free textural marks, delicate and coarse, transparent and opaque also support a vital center. Our own internal light breathes the texture of timelessness and wholeness into the powerful center.

“Pulsar Baby”
app18x40 inches (38x55.8cm)
DPI on hand-made paper

Inescapable Wholeness Texture

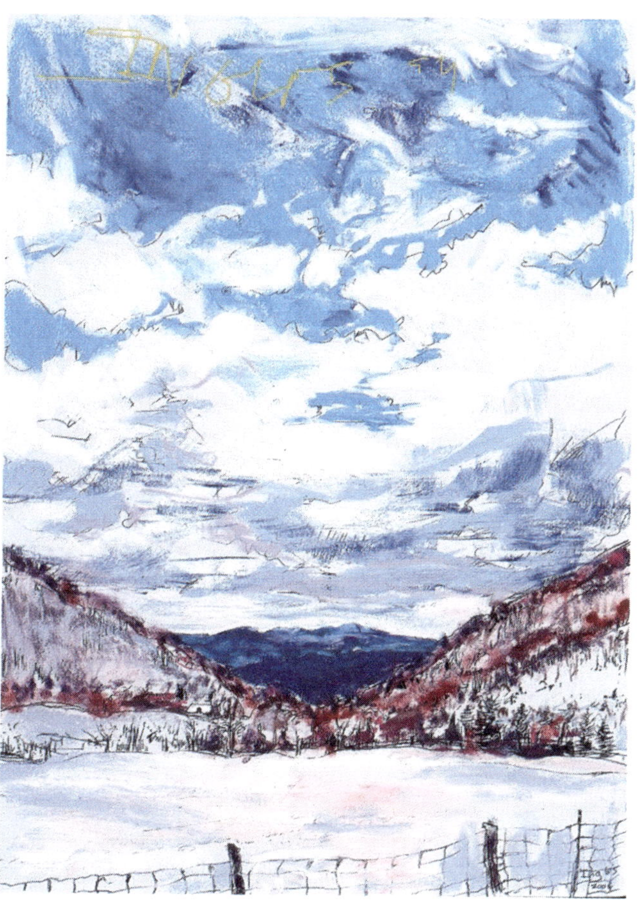

"Dunn's Gap"

Connection breathes through the living texture of "Dunn's Gap" because, even in winter, texture welcomes us to visit and stay awhile. Light created by texture sparks our memory of wholeness in Nature and the universe we live in together.

"Dunn's Gap, Winter Midday"
22x15 inches (55.8x38cm)
DPI, Conte pencil on printmaking paper

Signs of Sentient Life

I love to capture living light. I usually start by chasing sentient life. Living and seen. I see vital energy in shape, mass, and form. Quickening of Life. Existence inspirited. Expanding possibility, sentient life animates a field of vision. Smaller strong centers supported by multiple signs of sentient Life.

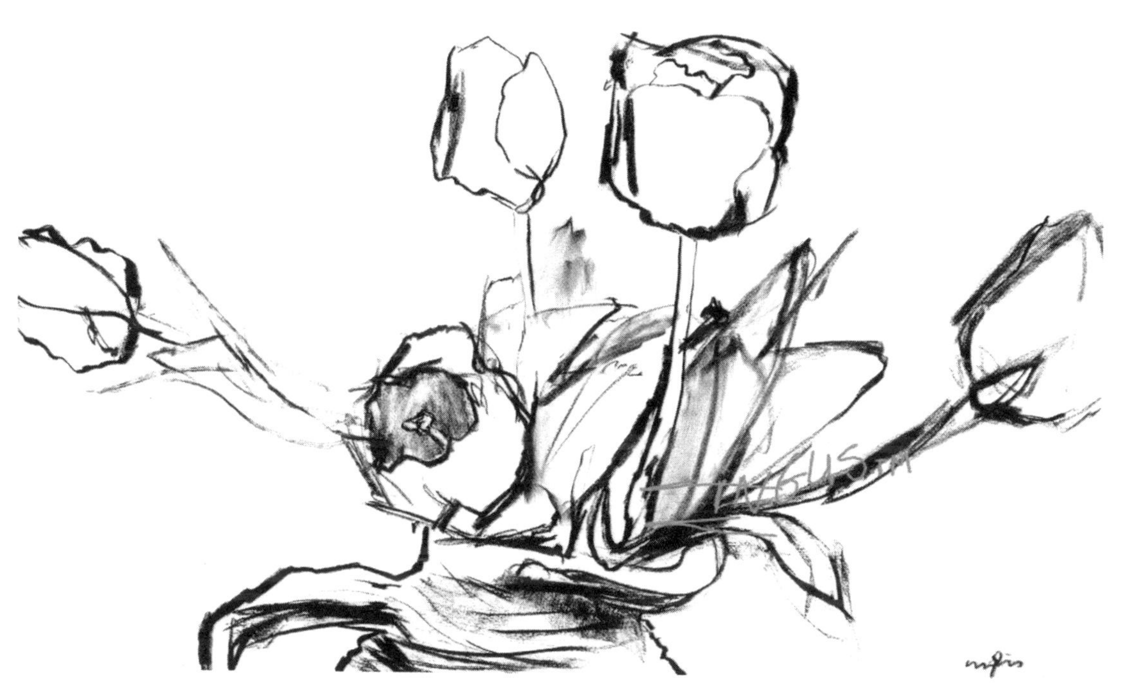

Sentient Life in the Moment

"Chelsea Tulips"

The center of beauty is strongly supported by a "volume of life" we feel in the oversized tulips. Sentient Life takes time to explore as the strong center suspends us.

"Chelsea Tulips"
22x30 inches (55.8x76cm)
Charcoal on printmaking paper

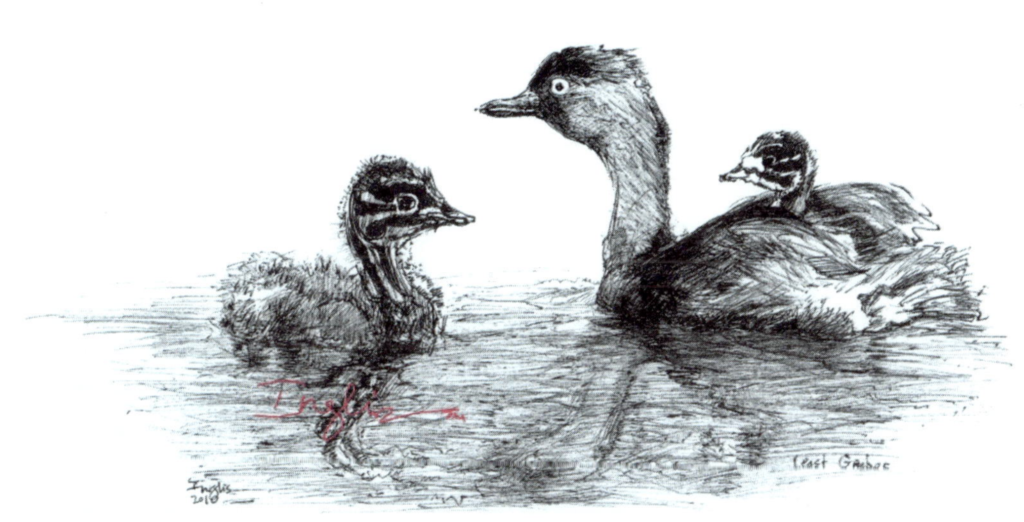

"Mother Grebe and Fledglings"

Life in the center of the drawing has something to do with all three ducks' lines-of-sight. Each exists in magnificent harmony with the other, vital to life. Their physical, sentient relationship to each other creates a center of life in the composition. The beauty that emanates from the mother and her two chicks charges the center of the drawing for us.

“Mother Grebe and Fledglings”
8x10 inches (20.3x25.4cm)
Ink on printmaking paper

Sentient Life Memory

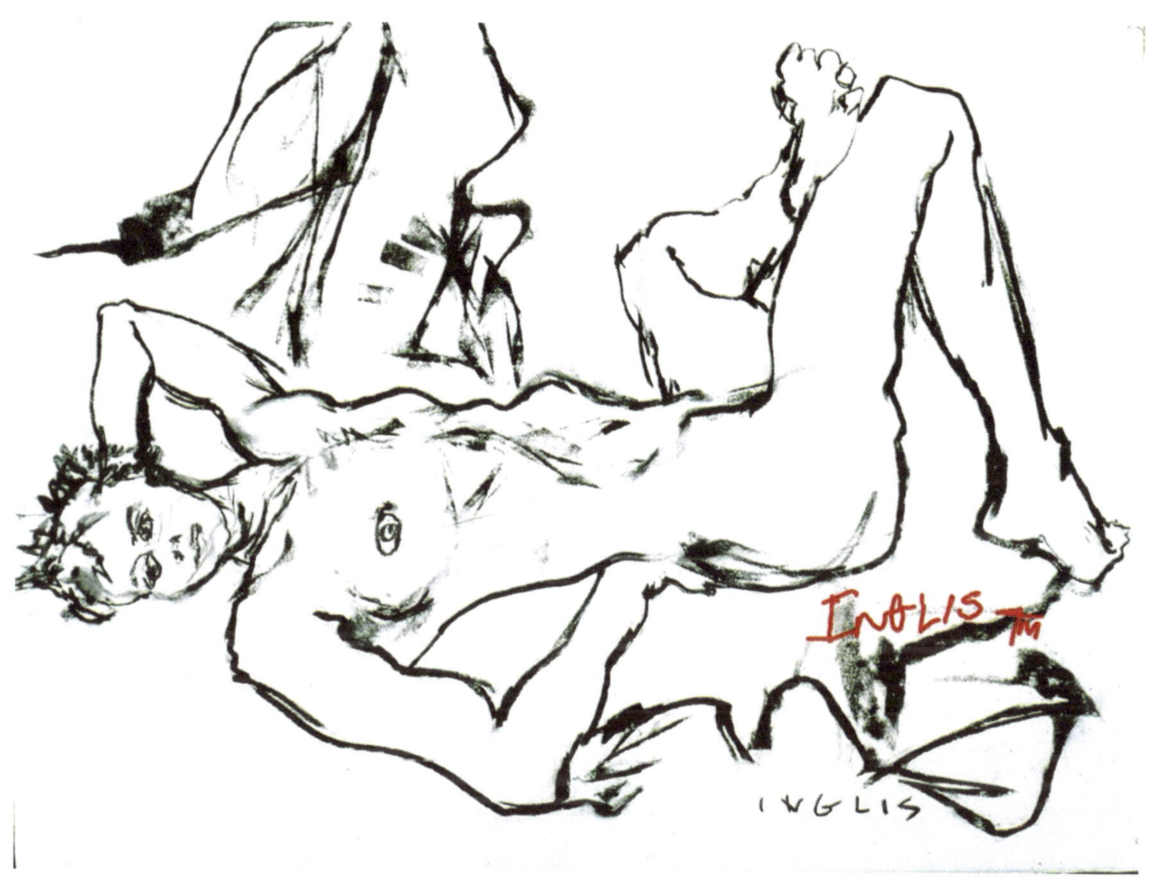

"Mariana, the Great"

Memory of vital energy inspires connection to the force of life. Physical and visual power in balance with a quiet wholeness in the Center. Positive space stimulates wholeness of sentient form. Potent texture empowers the smaller centers to support the whole life of the drawing. Looking for "living light" in Mariana: I found grace and power in vulnerability.

“Mariana, the Great”
22x30 inches (55.8x76cm)
Charcoal on printmaking paper

Strong Contrast

Successful contrast operates as harmony. Beautiful contrast can be found where power is entirely transparent and in equal proportion to natural vulnerability. Unity and Wholeness in Beauty occur when contrast inspires, connects, and strengthens the center and surrounding centers. Strong centers are made stronger with strategic contrast. Successful contrast can be very inspiring when all four elements—Line, Shape, Size, and Spacing—are vibrant and distinct, in balance.

Physical Contrast

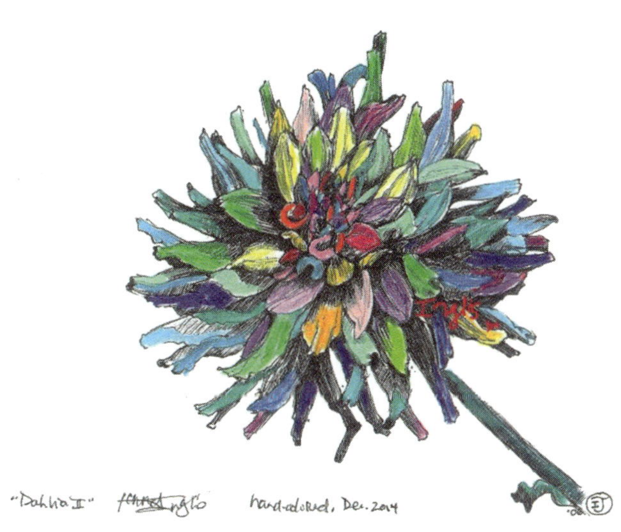

"Virginia Dahlia"

Deep shadow and highlights support strong physical contrast. Line, shape, size, and spacing create dynamic contrast between physical mass and space. The actual weight of the flower. And air space. Light and contrast strengthen the Center.

“Virginia Dahlia”
8x10 inches (20.3x25.4cm)
Ink on printmaking paper

Felt Contrast

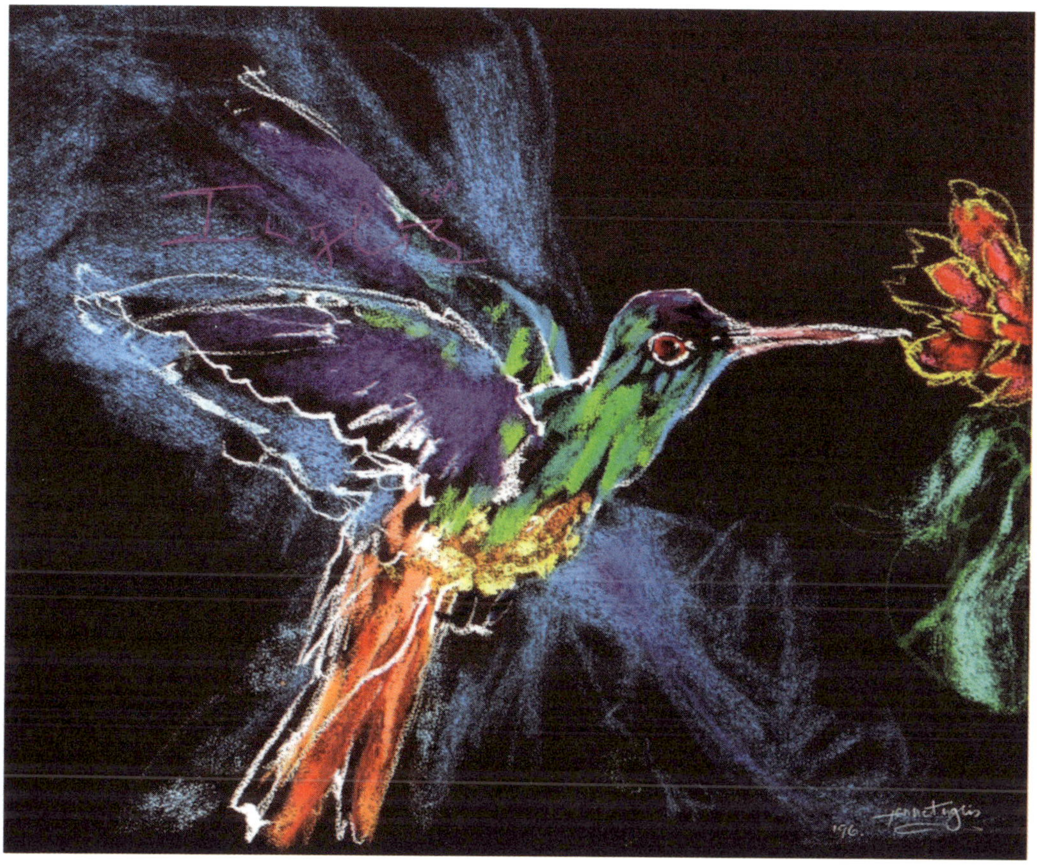

"Summer Nectar"

Here, contrast inspires, connects, and strengthens surrounding centers. The heart of the hummingbird is the Center. Contrast is made stronger by solid form in direct contrast with the dissolving of form. The stillness of the eye in contrast to the wings whose solidity evaporates, continuously. Felt contrast of life and death, vulnerability and scale. This hummingbird is 8 inches (20.3cm) head to tail; many others I've painted are in the 30-inch scale, all utilizing contrast for dramatic effect.

“Summer Nectar”
Private collection. New York, NY
15x18 inches (38x45.7cm)
Charcoal on printmaking paper

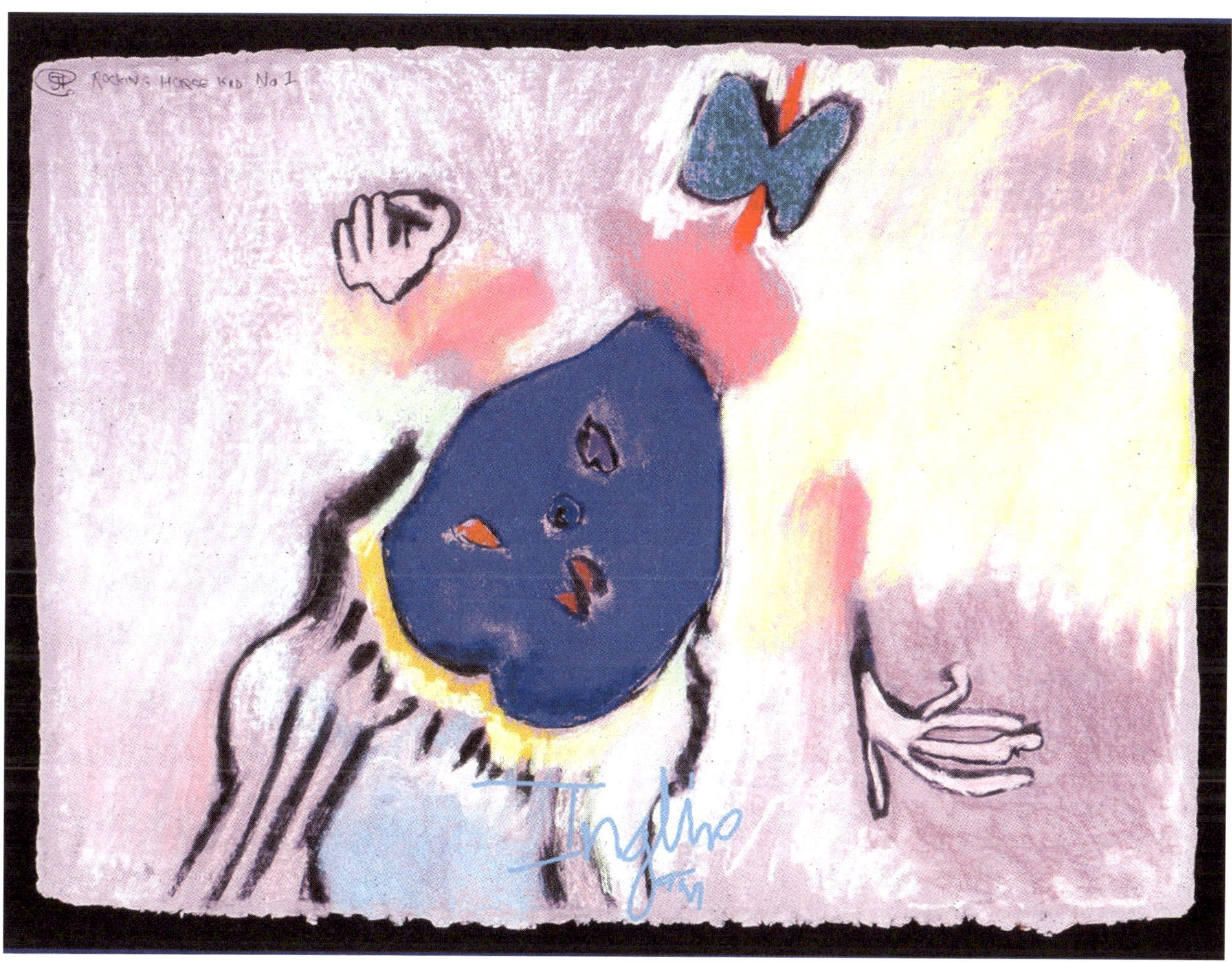

"Rocking Horse Kid"

"Rocking Horse Kid" is a self-portrait. There's a whole series, a family of Rocking Horse Kids. As portraits, felt contrast is raw and spontaneous. Life continuously reignites itself. Unity and separation are in play. Strong contrast animates, connects, and strengthens the Center.

“Rocking Horse Kid”
Private collection. Dusseldorf, Germany
18x24 inches (45.7x60.9cm)
DPI on hand-made paper

Borders and Edges

Borders and edges create fields with strong living centers. Both separating and unifying, borders create a pause, a limit, and a rest for the eye. Line, shape, size, and spacing are all animated by borders. Not rigidly defined or confined, but made more tangible and potent. Borders and Edges give meaning to a center in relation to its surroundings. A spatial void is also made more potent by strategic edges.

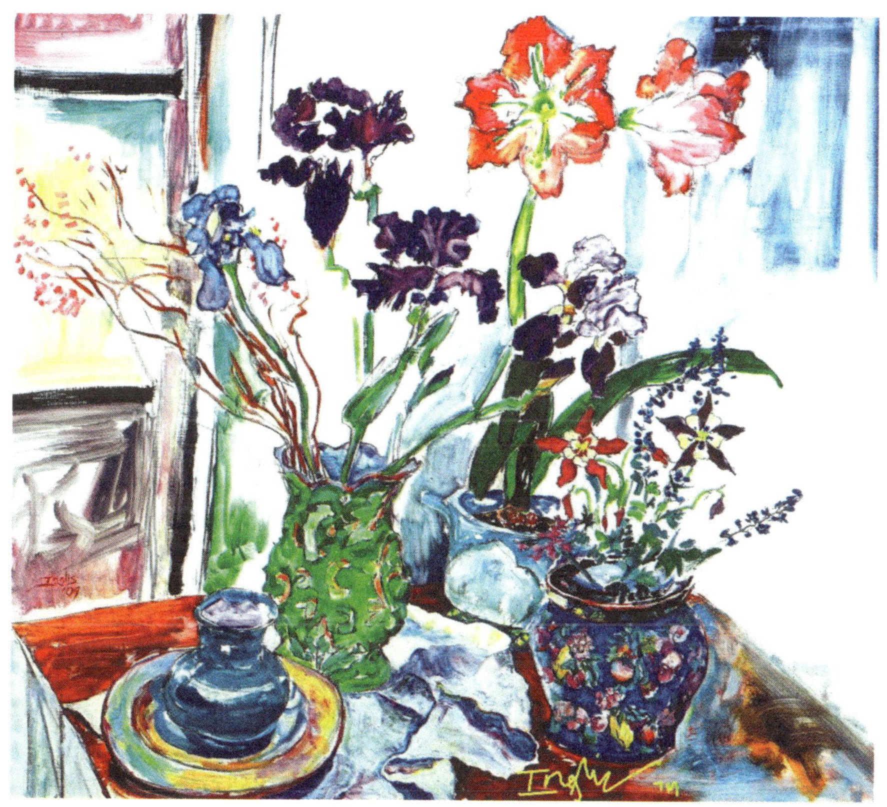

"Amaryllis, Iris, and Columbine"

Powerful borders and edges feed spatial vitality and dynamism. Architecture and organization add strength to living borders and living edges. Repetitive patterns strengthen a calming harmony.

“Amaryllis, Iris, Columbine”
Private collection.
30x36 inches (76x91.4cm)
Oil pigment on board

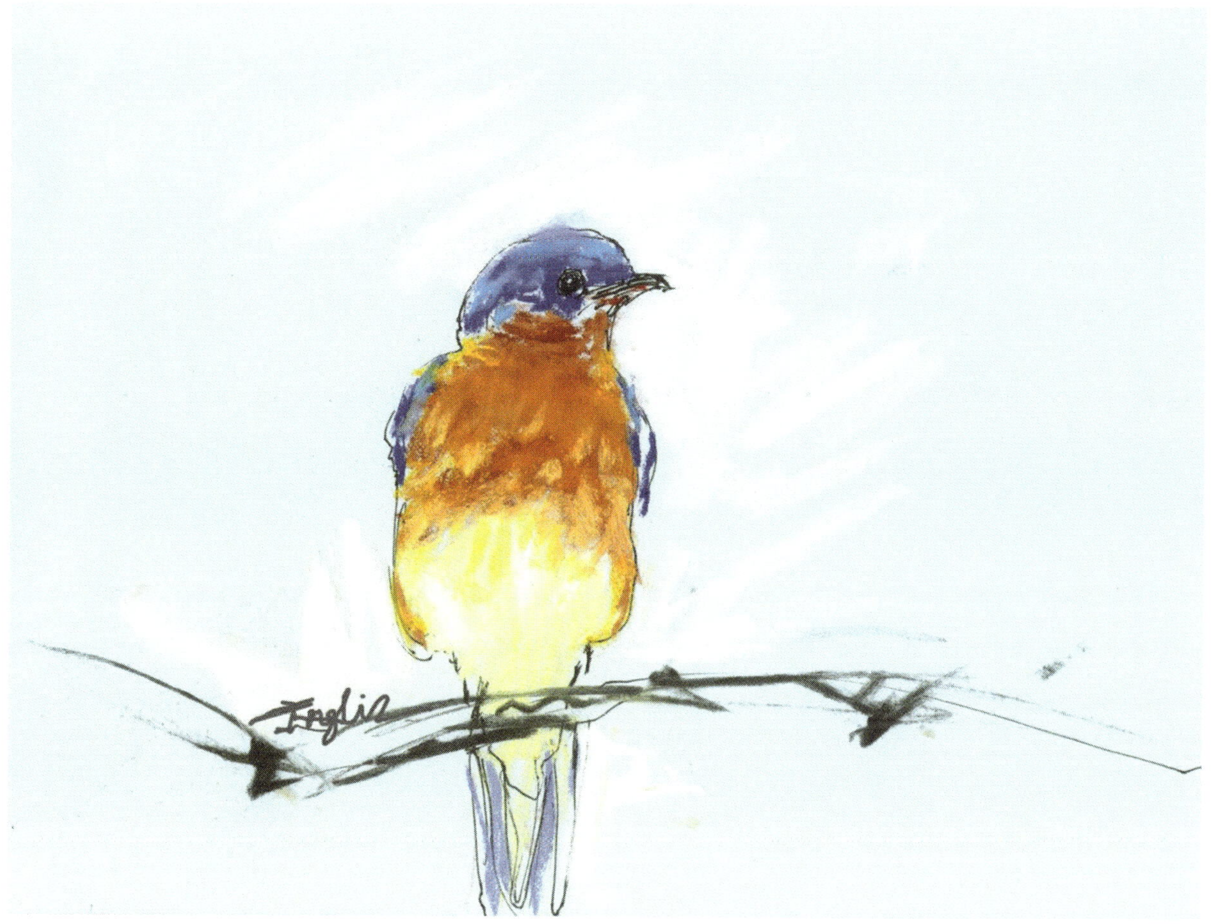

"solo blue boy"

Carefully crafted edges everywhere return our eyes to the heart of the bird. Ignoring that he is virtually floating in space, our friend is held confidently on his page. Mass and form explode with life in direct proportion to the dynamism of the four edges of the paper, namely the first border and edge. The bluebird himself seems held together by the breath of the Center.

“solo blue boy”
8x10 inches (20.3x25.4cm)
DPI on printmaking paper

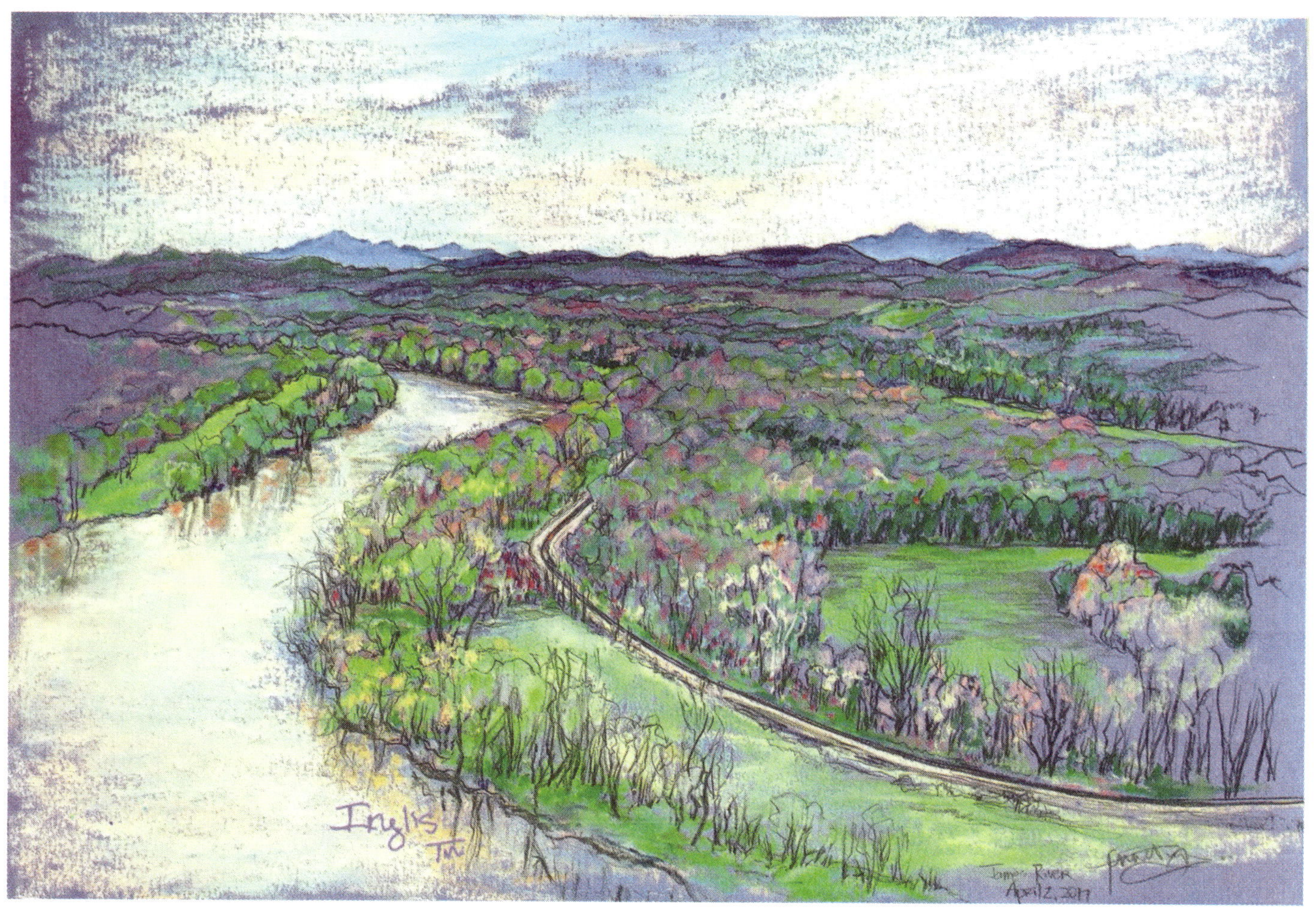

"April, James River"

Infinity calls in the Center. Deep horizons change how we see ourselves., they always do. We restore ourselves as we create a breathing picture plane in our mind's eye. Your eyes naturally careen in figure eight movements, up and down all around inside a "tube" of fore shortening, The business (tube) of foreshortening is convincingly effective with a powerful center, housed within 4 edges, and guided by the natural borders of the great river.

"April, James River"
15x22 inches (38x55.8cm)
DPI, Conte pencil, on watercolor paper

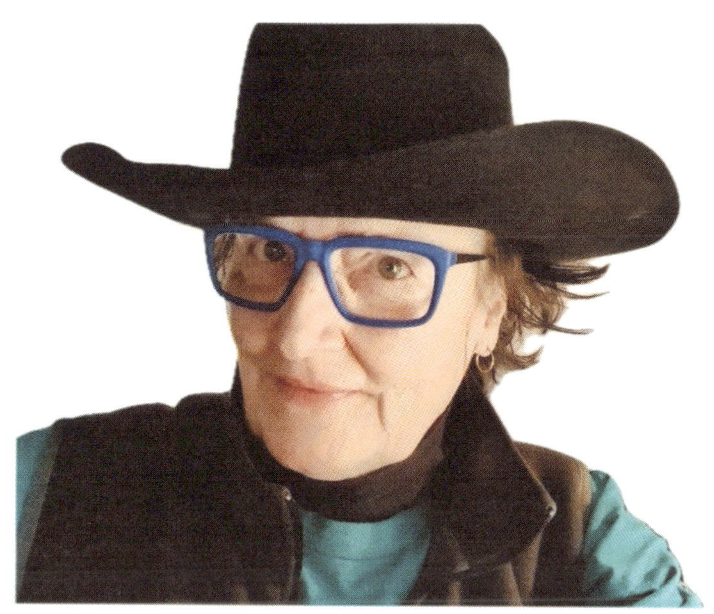

http://www.jennetinglis.com
http://www.masterinaminute.com
instagram @inglisgallery
facebook Inglis Art

Jennet Inglis Bio

Friends and colleagues refer to me as a creative savant. I am often told I must be superhuman, when it's simply genius autism. I used to cover up my autism because I felt unsafe being myself. But my thousands of paintings speak for me, so I can't deny who I really am. My world seems to slide through space at a different speed and amperage than those around me. One perception of myself is that ALL Time physically resides in me.

One of my first memories is being in a stroller in Manhattan when my mother stopped at a corner flower market. My face was pressed into those flowers, while my eyes were filled with their colors and shapes. I still remember those flowers, which is partly why I had to create these coloring books: to share with you my joy in nature.

My autism gives me a purpose, which is to inspire future generations. To that end, I have developed several public installation projects that synthesize Science, Art, and Spirit. I am grateful that my work has been exhibited nationally and internationally. I am often told that my work profoundly affects others. I have also been told, over and over again, that my projects will make a difference. So, here it is! I'm coming for you!

COMING SOON!

From the Master in a Minute® Series:

#2 Raptors

#3 Orchids, Dahlias, and More

#4 Horses

#5 Sunflowers 2